Special Needs in the Classroom: a Teacher Education Guide

Special Needs in the Classroom
A Teacher Education Guide

Mel Ainscow

Education on the move

UNESCO Publishing

C

371.9
·A 56
2004

The designations employed and the presentation of material throughout this publication do not imply the expression of any opinion whatsoever on the part of UNESCO concerning the legal status of any country, territory, city or area or its authorities, or concerning the delimitation of its frontiers or boundaries.

First edition published in the United Kingdom in 1994
by Jessica Kingsley Publishers Ltd and UNESCO

Second revised edition published by
The United Nations Educational,
Scientific and Cultural Organization
7 Place de Fonteroy
75732 Paris 07-SP, France

Typeset by Franck Tournel
Printed by Darantiere, 21801 Quetigny

ISBN 92-3-103952-0

Printed in France

Preface

UNESCO's mission in promoting Education for All and inclusion is clearly set out in the World Declaration on Education for All adopted by the World Conference on Education for All (Jomtien, Thailand, 1990) and in the Salamanca Statement on Principles, Policy and Practice in Special Needs Education adopted by the World Conference on Special Needs Education (Salamanca, Spain, 1994). The Dakar Framework for Action welcomes the commitments made at major education conferences throughout the 1990s and urges the international community to continue working towards delivery on these goals (World Education Forum, Dakar, 2000).

The Salamanca Statement was prepared to emphasize that in order to reach the goal of Education For All (EFA), all learners must be catered for in all education systems. It called upon the international community, in particular the partners of the Education for All movement, to endorse the approach of inclusive schooling and called upon the International Labour Organization, UNESCO, the United Nations Children's Fund (UNICEF) and the World Health Organization (WHO) to strengthen their technical assistance inputs and to reinforce their cooperation and networking for more efficient support to expanded and integrated provision.

During the 1990s a number of very important works were produced and were subsequently instrumental in the promotion of inclusive approaches in education. Special Needs in the Classroom: A Teacher Education Guide as well as the Teacher Education Resource Pack are two of these. Both these publications have now been updated. We hope that these materials will continue to be of considerable value to the development of schools open to all children.

Special Needs in the Classroom has its origins in the UNESCO teacher education project of the same name and was prepared as a supplement to the Teacher Education Resource Pack. It is part of UNESCO's continuing work in encouraging Member States to develop strategies for responding to children's special needs in ordinary schools. It also reflects UNESCO's contribution to the efforts by various organizations to improve teacher education by helping teachers respond positively to all children likely to experience difficulties in school. This includes those who have particular disabilities as well as many others who for a variety of reasons do not make satisfactory progress.

While it is specifically intended for teacher educators using the Resource Pack, it is written so as to make it relevant and useful as a source of ideas for all those wishing to help teachers become more skilled in dealing with pupil diversity in mainstream schools.

UNESCO would like to express its gratitude to the author for his original work on this publication and for its updating. In preparing this work, Mel Ainscow has made considerable use of the ideas and experiences generated through regional and national workshops, sponsored largely by UNESCO. However, the author is responsible for the choice and presentation of the facts contained in this book and for the opinions expressed therein, which are not necessarily those of UNESCO and do not commit the Organization.

Contents

Acknowledgements

This book was written with the help and on behalf of an international resource team.

The members of the team are:

Anupam Ahuja	India
Mel Ainscow	United Kingdom
Cynthia Duk	Chile
Gerardo Echeita	Spain
Hala Ibrahim	Jordan
N K Jangira	India
Mennas Machawira	Zimbabwe
Chipo Marira	Zimbabwe
Charles Mifsud	Malta
Joseph Mifsud	Malta
Sophia Ngaywa	Kenya
Winston Rampaul	Canada
Chris Rose	Canada
Lena Saleh	UNESCO, Paris
Nina Sotorrio	Spain
Danielle Van Steenlandt	Chile
Grace Wang'ombe	Kenya
Zuhair Zakaria	Jordan

The team acknowledges the contributions of teachers and teacher educators from many countries throughout the world. The book is, therefore, a tribute to a remarkable example of international collaboration in which colleagues from different cultures have worked together in the interests of all children.

Mel Ainscow
Cambridge, England

Introduction

This guide book was developed as a result of research associated with the UNESCO teacher education project, 'Special Needs in the Classroom'. The aim of the project was to design and disseminate a Resource Pack of teacher education materials. This guide book provides the following:

1. Theoretical and practical ideas that will be of value to teacher educators involved in both pre-service and in-service teacher education.
2. An account of the development of the UNESCO Resource Pack, 'Special Needs in the Classroom', outlining the processes of international collaboration that led to its design and the research that has informed its model of dissemination.
3. Detailed accounts of ways in which the Resource Pack might be used, including an account of its theoretical rationale and instructions that will provide the basis of training for teacher educators.

The guide is specifically intended to be used by those using the Resource Pack. However it is written in such a way as to make it relevant and useful as a source of ideas for all teacher educators wishing to help teachers become more skilled in dealing with pupil diversity in mainstream schools. We hope it will also encourage some readers to use the Resource Pack.

In this Introduction we provide an outline of the context that led to the UNESCO project. In particular we present an account of the problems and issues facing school systems in different parts of the world as they seek to respond to all children in their communities. The Introduction concludes with an overview of the chapters in the book.

THE INTERNATIONAL SCENE

It is beyond doubt that across the world many children do not receive adequate education, including large numbers who have disabilities. This is so despite the fact that it is now more than forty years since the nations of the world, speaking through the Universal Declaration of Human Rights, asserted that 'everyone has a right to education'.

The text of the 1990 World Conference on Education for All, held in Thailand, pointed out that the following realities persist:

- More that one hundred million children, including at least sixty million girls, have no access to primary schooling.
- More than nine hundred and sixty million adults, two-thirds of whom are women, are illiterate, and functional illiteracy is a significant problem in all countries, industrialized and developing.
- More than one-third of the world's adults have no access to the printed knowledge, new skills, and technologies that could improve the quality of their lives and help them shape, and adapt to, social and cultural change.
- More than one hundred million children and countless adults fail to complete basic education programmes; millions more satisfy the attendance requirements but do not acquire essential knowledge and skills.

The contribution of the field of special education has, therefore, to be considered against this background of international crisis with respect to education in general.

Probably the most helpful source of data with respect to special educational provision internationally arises out of a survey of fifty-eight countries conducted in 1986–87 (UNESCO 1988b). The information provided by this survey illustrates the discrepancies in the level of progress among the various regions and countries. It was found, for example, that thirty-four of the countries had fewer than 1 per cent of pupils enrolled in special educational programmes; ten of these countries had special education provision available for less than one-tenth of one per cent of pupils.

Precise figures for developing countries are particularly difficult to establish, but the studies that are available confirm the disturbing scale of the problem. For example, Ross (1988) summarized data gathered from thirteen countries in eastern and southern Africa indicating that virtually all these countries had special education enrolments for approximately 0.1 per cent or fewer of the school population. Such data led Hegarty (1990) to conclude:

The stark reality underlying these figures is that the great majority of children and young people with disabilities do not receive an appropriate education – if indeed they are offered any education. In many countries, less than one child in a hundred receives the special educational provision that she/he needs (p. 4).

PATTERNS OF DEVELOPMENT

It is possible to detect certain patterns in the historical development of special education across different countries. The pace of this development varies, of course, from country to country. It is also important to note that the field of special education is of relatively recent origin. In its early stages the emphasis was on provision for children with distinct disabilities, but with the expansion of public education in many countries, broader forms of special education have been introduced.

An example of this pattern of development can be seen in the United Kingdom where the first schools for the blind and deaf were founded towards the end of the eighteenth century. The first separate education provision for children with physical disabilities was made in 1851, and before the middle of the nineteenth century so-called mentally defective children were often placed in workhouses and infirmaries. Special provision for pupils with milder forms of disability was to come much later.

As with ordinary education, education for children with disabilities in many countries began with individual and charitable enterprise. Government intervention followed, first to support voluntary efforts, and finally to create a national framework in which public and voluntary agencies could act in partnership to see that all children receive a suitable education. In many developing countries such a national framework has still to be established (UNESCO 1988a).

Many of the current practices of special education have developed since the early 1960s. This period has been marked by significant shifts in beliefs within the field and, indeed, this process of change is still apparent in many parts of the world.

During the early part of that period there was a marked emphasis on making provision for children with particular disabilities. In many countries special education provision was dependent upon a process of assessment leading to a child being categorized with respect to a perceived handicapping condition. Thus, over the years, special education came to see itself – and to be seen by others – as a separate world catering for that small population of the child population perceived as being disabled. Those involved in special education had relatively little contact with mainstream schools. This tendency to isolation was reinforced in some countries by the fact that many of the providers of special education were voluntary organizations and that some special schools were located in accommodation away from the community.

The latter 1960s and early 1970s began to see considerable changes in emphasis. A concern with equal opportunities in a number of Western countries heightened awareness of children in ordinary schools who were perceived as making unsatisfactory progress. Consequently there was a substantial growth in various forms of remedial education, including the establishment of special classes within, or attached to, mainstream schools.

RECENT DEVELOPMENTS

The 1970s saw further changes in many countries. New ideas were emerging that were to challenge the basis of existing provision for pupils now commonly referred to as having special educational needs. Adams (1986) summarized six particularly important trends. These were:

1. A growing understanding that handicapping conditions are much more widely spread, more varied and more complex than systems of categorization based largely on medical criteria tend to indicate.
2. Greater awareness that not only does the incidence of handicap and our recognition of it alter over time as a result of medical, economic and social changes, but also that the difficulties encountered by young people in their educational and general development are likely to arise as much from disadvantageous circumstances as from individual characteristics.

3. More general acceptance of the fact that parents, however much in some cases they may be 'part of the problem', not only have rights in relation to their children which must be respected, but also have a unique and uniquely valuable contribution to make to their children's development which must be more effectively exploited by the professionals.
4. A growing recognition of the value – indeed in many instances the crucial importance – of very early intervention to help children with special needs and of the need for continuing attention with regular review and appropriate modification of support programmes to meet their changing needs.
5. A better appreciation of the fact that there is no sharp divide between 'handicapped' and 'normal', but rather a range of individual needs across a continuum.
6. Wider understanding and acceptance of the fact that every young person has a right to as full, independent and 'normal' a life as possible and that, therefore, the aim of the community in relation to young people with more severe difficulties must be as much integration as possible into the mainstream of school and community life.

As a result of these trends significant legislation to change the basis of special education was introduced in a number of countries. Possibly the most influential of these was Public Law 94-142, the 'Education for All Handicapped Children Act' (1975), in the United States. This sought a legislative solution to educational inequities in that it was designed to redress the 'de facto denial of the rights to education of the handicapped' (Yanok 1986). The key provision was the requirement that state schools throughout the country should provide appropriate education for every school-age child, irrespective of the nature of the child's disability. More specifically, the legislation mandated that all students with disabilities be provided with appropriate instruction in the least restrictive environment possible, which for most would be in the regular classroom. It also specified an elaborate set of procedures and timelines for referral, assessment, classification and placement of students, and extended to students and parents certain constitutional rights and procedural safeguards (Skrtic 1991b).

The American legislation has subsequently inspired similar developments in other Western countries. For example, the 1981 'Education

Act' in England and Wales sought to establish a new framework for children requiring special provision. Its main strategy was the introduction of the 'Statement of Special Educational Need', an extensive reporting procedure used to monitor the progress of individual pupils and, where necessary, provide them with additional resources. This legislation shares broadly similar approaches to those required by the American legislation.

Evidence of new legislation internationally is provided by a 1980s survey (UNESCO 1988b). Two thirds of the respondents in the survey (i.e., thirty-eight out of fifty-eight countries) made reference to new legislation under discussion or being introduced. This ranged from loosely formulated discussions of the need for various legislative developments to definite plans to introduce regulations governing specific aspects of educational provision.

THE ISSUE OF INTEGRATION

Evidence from the UNESCO survey (1988b) indicates that the predominant form of provision for special education in many parts of the world is in separate special schools. But such schools often serve very limited numbers of children, leaving many children with disabilities with little or no education. These observations led the participants in UNESCO's consultation in special education (1988a) to make the following statement:

> Given the size of the demand and the limited resources available, the education and training needs of the majority of disabled persons cannot be met by special schools and centres (p. 15).

Consequently, a way forward will require changes in both special and mainstream schools. Mainstream schools have to develop forms of organization and teaching that cater for greater pupil diversity; while those special schools that do exist must develop an outward looking stance and take on significantly new roles (Hegarty 1990).

There is considerable evidence that in many countries throughout the world integration is a central element in planning of special education (e.g. Ainscow 1990; Pijl and Meijer 1991; UNESCO 1988b).

Such an emphasis seems sensible for Third World countries given the extent of the need and the inevitable limitations of available resources. It is also important to note that in many developing countries substantial 'casual' integration of children with disabilities in ordinary schools occurs (Miles 1989).

In considering the current scene internationally with respect to integration, however, we come up against differences of definition. Pijl and Meijer (1991) use the term integration as a collective noun for all attempts to avoid a segregated and isolated education for pupils with disabilities. As a result of their survey of policies for integration in eight Western countries, they suggest that its scope can range from the actual integration of regular and special schools (or classes) to measures for reducing the outflow of students from regular education to special education. Consequently, it becomes very difficult to quantify the numbers of pupils with special needs who receive their education in integrated settings, particularly if the important distinction is made between social and curricular integration.

Developed countries are experiencing their own difficulties in establishing effective policies for integration. The existence of well-established separate provision in special schools and classes creates complex policy dilemmas leading many countries to operate what Pijl and Meijer (1991) refer to as 'two tracks'. In other words, these countries have parallel but separate segregation and integration policies.

In some countries integration represents an aspiration for the future. In Germany, for example, while some pilot initiatives based on the idea of integration are underway, students who are declared eligible for special education must be placed in a special school. Statistics for 1986 showed that 4.2 per cent of all students aged between six and sixteen were in separate schools for special education. On the other hand, some countries (for example, Denmark, Norway and Spain) have shown considerable progress in implementing the integration principle universally. Here the local community school is often seen as the normal setting for pupils with special needs.

Discrepancies between stated policy and actual practice are evident in many countries. For example, Pijl and Meijer (1991) note that despite the fact that special schools were abolished in Italy in 1977, most of the so-called integrated pupils are 'integrated outside the classroom'. Often this means that they are taught by support teachers in separate classrooms. It is reported that the reasons for problems in implementing a policy of integration are that regular school teachers still do not regard the teaching of pupils with special needs as their responsibility and are often not equipped (with training and materials) to do so.

A problem reported from a number of industrialized countries is that despite national policies emphasizing integration, there is evidence of a significant increase in the proportions of pupils being categorized and given separate placements in order that their schools can earn additional resources (Ainscow 1991). As a result of her analysis of policies in Australia, England and Scandinavia, and the United States, Fulcher (1989) suggests that the increased bureaucracy that is often associated with special education, and the inevitable struggles that go on for additional resources, have the effect of escalating the proportion of school children labelled as disabled.

Dissatisfaction with progress towards integration has caused demands for more radical changes in policy in a number of countries (Ainscow 1991). In the United States this has led to the Regular Education Initiative, a movement calling for the merger of special and regular education (Wang *et al.* 1986; Will 1986; Stainback and Stainback 1984b). A thorough critical analysis of this development and the heated debate that it has created in the United States is provided by Skrtic (1991b).

INTERNATIONAL ACTIVITIES

Since the International Year of Disabled Persons (1981) there has been considerable international collaboration with respect to the development of special education policies and programmes. Organizations such as UNESCO, the United Nations Children's Fund (UNICEF), and the Organization for Economic Co-operation and Development (OECD) have acted to encourage collaborative developments and many national agencies have invested resources to give them support. The World Declaration on Education for All adopted by the World Conference on Education for All (Jomtein, 1990) gives further impetus to these efforts. Specifically, in Article 3.5, it states:

> The learning needs of the disabled demand special attention. Steps need to be taken to provide equal access to education to every category of disabled persons as an integral part of the education system.

This challenge is enormous, particularly in developing countries.

Preferred ways of conducting international efforts remain a matter of debate. For example, Miles (1989) is doubtful of the value of introducing Western models of special education into countries such as Pakistan and India. He suggests that the reasons that they often do not seem to work are complex but include what he refers to as 'conceptual blockage'. He notes that Western special education is constructed on views of children and schooling that may be largely alien to much of the population of the Indian subcontinent. Furthermore, he is critical of the work of advisers visiting Third World countries as part of what he characterizes as the 'Western conceptual crusade' that seems to ignore the realities of Third World situations.

At the International Consultation of Special Education (UNESCO 1988a) participants reviewed and assessed international developments related to special education over the previous decade. They also made suggestions concerning the focus of actions to be taken. Conscious of the magnitude of the problems and committed to the principles of normalization, integration, and participation, they recommended the complementary approaches of community-based rehabilitation and integrated education as the most effective ways forward.

Community-based rehabilitation (CBR) is being used by an increasing number of developing countries as a strategy to eliminate the constraints of institution-based rehabilitation. Its implementation in a particular context will depend to a large degree upon a country's strategies for socio-economic development. Often countries start by setting up a CBR project in a selected district, which provides the basis for gaining national experience and expertise. This is followed later by the launching of a wider programme, possibly as part of a national plan. Werner (1987) provides an impressive manual of suggestions for setting up such initiatives in rural communities, including examples of child-to-child activities. These are intended to encourage school-age children to help their disabled peers. It is interesting to note that these approaches, developed for use in Third World contexts, mirror some of the techniques now being used to create inclusive schools in the West (e.g. Lipsky and Gartner 1989). In particular both emphasize collaboration, including co-operative learning approaches, as a means of utilizing existing resources for the purposes of problem solving in educational contexts.

The UNESCO survey (1988b) presents a gloomy picture with respect to the international scene in teacher preparation. Only a minority of the fifty-eight countries reported coverage of disability issues in pre-service training programmes for all teachers. In-service training opportunities for teachers in regular schools were similarly limited. A wide range of training opportunities were reported for teachers specializing in special education – a five-year course in a teachers college at one extreme, to on-the-job instruction offered on an *ad hoc* basis at the other.

While it is difficult to generalize across widely diverse countries, it seems clear that the main thrust of training at present is directed at specialists who will work in segregated special schools. However, it can be argued that the vast majority of children with disabilities, and many others who experience difficulties, could be helped in mainstream schools by relatively minor adjustments to the teaching that is provided (Hegarty 1990). Thus an investment in the pre-service preparation of teachers with respect to strategies for accommodating pupil diversity could bring about major improvements in the special education provision offered by schools.

PROBLEMS AND ISSUES

From this summary of international developments with respect to the education of children and youth said to have special needs, it is possible to draw out a number of important problems and issues that require urgent attention. While in its relatively short existence the field of special education has made much progress, an analysis of the current scene around the world presents a disturbing picture. Hegarty (1990) sums up the situation:

> Those with disabilities, who ironically have the greatest need of education, are the least likely to receive it. This is true of developed and developing countries alike. (p. 2)

In developed countries many pupils with disabilities, and others who fail to achieve satisfactory progress in school learning, are formally excluded from the mainstream education system or receive less favourable treatment within it than do other children. On the other hand, in many developing countries the continuing struggle to achieve compulsory education for a majority of children takes precedence over meeting the needs of those with disabilities.

The UNESCO Consultation on Special Education (UNESCO 1988a) outlined a number of general obstacles to improvement. These are:

- Inadequacy of perceptions and thus in policy formation which is very much linked to attitudes, whether they be cultural, religious, political, or ideological.
- Rigidity in legislative and administrative provision, especially in relation to rigid characterization of disability and categorical allocation of resources often not matched to individual needs.
- The discrepancy between what exists and our present knowledge of what should exist due to poor dissemination of knowledge.
- Special education in some countries is still perceived as a charitable venture – a welfare programme. Responsibility for special education is not always with educational authorities.
- The administrative and professional separation that continues to divide the educational community into 'special' and 'regular' components isolated from each other.

As the field of special education internationally continues to seek an appropriate way forward, there has recently emerged from within its own ranks a new set of voices arguing for further reform. Once again these voices reflect developments in different parts of the world. While inevitably they are not in full agreement with respect to their analysis and recommendations, they all adopt a critical perspective, seeking to question the field's theories and assumptions. Examples of writers sharing this perspective include in Australia, Fulcher (1989); in the United Kingdom, Tomlinson (1982); in New Zealand, Ballard (1990); in Papua New Guinea, Carrier (1983); and in the United States, Skrtic (1991). They all draw on theories from outside special education, such as sociology, politics, philosophy and organizational analysis. Their work, and that of others adopting similar stances, offers a more radical analysis of the policy and practice of special education pointing to new possibilities for reform.

One of their concerns is with the way in which pupils within schools come to be designated as having special needs. They see this as a social process that needs to be continually challenged. More specifically, they argue that the continued emphasis on explaining educational difficulties in terms of child-centred characteristics has the effect of preventing progress in the field. The argument is summed up by Dyson (1990) who states:

> The fact remains that the education system as a whole, and the vast majority of institutions and teachers within it, are approaching the twenty-first century with a view of special needs the same as that with which their counterparts approached the present century. That view, for all its avowed concern for the individual child, promotes injustice on a massive scale. It demands to be changed (p. 60–1).

This radical perspective leads to a reconceptualization of the special needs task (Ainscow 1991). This suggests that progress in the field is dependent upon a general recognition that difficulties experienced by pupils come about as a result of the way schools are organized and the forms of teaching that are provided. In other words, as Skrtic (1991) puts it, students with special needs are artefacts of the traditional curriculum.

INCLUSIVE EDUCATION

All of this has helped to encourage an interest in a new orientation, that of inclusive education. This adds yet further complications and disputes to those that already exist. Driven, in part at least, by ideological considerations, the idea of inclusive education challenges much of existing thinking in the special needs field, whilst, at the same time, offering a critique of the practices of general education. Put simply, many of those who are supporting the idea are raising the question, *why is it that schools throughout the world fail to teach so many pupils successfully?*

All of this suggests that the issue of inclusion must be seen within the context of the wider international discussions of 'Education for All', as stimulated by the 1990 World Conference held in Jomtien, Thailand. During the years since Jomtien thinking in the field has moved on. At the World Forum on Education For All in Dakar, April 2000, it was acknowledged that many groups of children continue to be marginalised within EFA campaigns, particularly those from minority ethnic groups and those with 'special learning needs', despite the targets set for the achievement of basic education for all at the Jomtien Conference. In paragraph 19 of the notes associated with the Dakar Framework for Action it is argued:

The key challenge is to ensure that the broad vision of Education for All as an inclusive concept is reflected in national government and funding agency policies.

So, instead of an emphasis on the idea of *integration,* with its assumption that additional arrangements will be made to accommodate pupils seen as being special within a system of schooling that remains largely unchanged, we now see moves towards *inclusive education,* where the aim is to restructure schools in response to the needs of all pupils.

The inclusive orientation is a strong feature of The Salamanca Statement on Principles, Policy and Practice in Special Needs Education, agreed by representatives of 92 governments and 25 international organisations in June 1994 (UNESCO, 1994). Arguably the most significant international document that has ever appeared in the special needs field, the Statement recommends that: 'Children with special educational needs must have access to regular schools which should accommodate them within a child-centred pedagogy capable of meeting these needs'. It goes on to argue that regular schools with an inclusive orientation are 'the most effective means of combating discriminatory attitudes, building an inclusive society and achieving education for all'. Furthermore, it suggests, such schools can 'provide an effective education for the majority of children and improve the efficiency and ultimately the cost-effectiveness of the entire education system'.

Implicit in this orientation is a paradigm shift in respect to the way we look at educational difficulties. This shift in thinking is based on the belief that methodological and organisational changes made in response to pupils experiencing difficulties can, under certain conditions, benefit all children. Within such a formulation those pupils who are currently categorised as having special needs come to be recognised as the stimulus that can encourage developments towards a richer overall learning environment.

Moves towards inclusion are also endorsed by the UN Convention on the Rights of the Child. Specifically the adoption of the Convention by the UN General Assembly and its subsequent ratification by 187 countries imposes a requirement for radical changes to traditional approaches to provision made for children with disabilities. The Convention contains a number of articles that require governments to undertake a systematic analysis of their laws, policies and practices in order to assess the extent to which they currently comply with the obligations they impose in respect to such children.

Article 28 of the Convention asserts the basis right of every child to education and requires that this should be provided on the basis of equality of opportunity. In other words the Convention allows no discrimination in relation to access to education on grounds of disability. Furthermore the continued justification of the types of segregated provision made in many countries needs to be tested against the child's rights not to be discriminated against, not least in that Articles 28 and 29, together with Articles 2, 3 and 23, seem to imply that all children have a right to inclusive education, irrespective of disability.

The UN Standard Rules for the Equalisation of Opportunities for Disabled Persons also has relevance (UN, 1993). Although not legally binding, it provides a globally recognised framework for the formulation of rights-based disability legislation by governments (Jones et al, 2002). Negotiations are currently underway for the development of a UN Convention on the Rights of Disabled People. Disabled people's organisations worldwide are leading the campaign for this new Convention in order to protect and promote their rights which continue to be violated, despite the international instruments which already exist.

Advancing towards the implementation of an inclusive orientation is far from easy, however, and evidence of progress is limited in most countries. Moreover, it must not be assumed that there is full acceptance of the inclusive philosophy. There are, for example, those who argue that small specialist units located in the standard school environment can provide the specialist knowledge, equipment and support for which the mainstream classroom and teacher can never provide a full substitute. On this view, such units may be the only way to provide feasible and effective access to education for certain groups of children.

In summary, then, as we look at how teacher education can encourage and support the development of schools that are effective in reaching vulnerable groups of children, it is necessary to recognise that the field itself is riddled with uncertainties, disputes and contradictions. However, what can be said is that throughout the world attempts are being made to provide more effective educational responses to such children, and that encouraged by the lead given by the Salamanca Statement, the overall trend is towards making these responses, as far as possible, within the context of general educational provision.

The new inclusive perspective is the one that was adopted and developed in the UNESCO project 'Special Needs in the Classroom'. It is based upon the view that the way forward must be to reform schools in ways that will make them respond positively to pupil diversity, seeing individual differences as something to be nurtured and celebrated. Within such a conceptualization, a consideration of difficulties experienced by pupils and teachers can provide an agenda for reform and, indeed, insights as to how this might be accomplished.

However, this kind of approach is only possible in schools where there exist a respect for individuality and a culture of collaboration that encourages and supports problem-solving. Such cultures are likely to facilitate the learning of all pupils and, alongside them, the professional learning of all teachers. Ultimately, therefore, this line of argument makes the case that increasing equity is the key to improvements in schooling for all.

THE ORIGINS OF THE UNESCO PROJECT

The initiative for the project 'Special Needs in the Classroom' grew out of UNESCO's continuing work in encouraging member countries to develop strategies for responding to children's special needs in ordinary schools. A survey of fourteen countries, commissioned by UNESCO and carried out by a research team from the University of London (Bowman 1986), identified three major priorities for development with respect to policy development:

1. The provision of compulsory education for all children in the population.
2. The integration of pupils with disabilities into ordinary schools.
3. The upgrading of teacher training as a means of achieving the first two priorities.

The findings of this survey were used as the basis of a series of regional workshops. An outcome of these events was that UNESCO was urged to assist in the dissemination of teacher-training materials that could be used to facilitate improvements with respect to meeting special needs in ordinary school. It was also recommended that seven points be kept in mind in carrying out this work:

1. The need to develop national policies for teacher education that progress in a continuous fashion from the pre-service stage through to the in-service stage.
2. The importance of supervised practical experience as a major element of teacher education programmes.
3. The importance of taking account of what has been referred to as the 'hidden population' of pupils with special needs. These are children who do not have significant disabilities but who nevertheless experience difficulties in learning. (The original survey, for example, indicated that up to 45 per cent of pupils repeated one or more grades in some countries.)
4. A necessity to increase flexibility of curriculum practice and teaching methods in mainstream classrooms in order to be more responsive to the needs of individual children.
5. The principle of self-help brought about by encouraging teachers to develop skills of self-evaluation as a means of developing their practice.
6. The importance of recognizing the value of collaboration amongst groups of teachers within a school.
7. The need to help and encourage teachers to make better use of three sources of non-professional help in the classroom: the pupils themselves; parents, relatives and others in the community; and paid ancillary help or teachers' aides.

The regional workshops also generated some more specific recommendations regarding the possible content of teacher education programmes.

Consequently, in 1988 the author was invited to direct a project to be called 'Special Needs in the Classroom' that would aim to develop and disseminate a resource pack of education materials.

Clearly, the design of suitable teacher-education materials represented an enormous challenge. In particular, there was the issue of how to produce a pack that could take account of such a wide range of national contexts, especially those in developing countries. A number of measures were taken during the formulation of the materials in an attempt to achieve a level of flexibility that could take account of diverse settings. These were as follows:

1. Advisory teams consisting of teacher educators and teachers were created in different parts of the world. These teams provided comment on draft materials and contributed materials and ideas of their own for inclusion in the pack.
2. A number of special educators, and others involved in teacher development, around the world read and commented upon draft materials.
3. A pilot workshop for teachers and teacher educators from various African countries was held in Nairobi, Kenya in April 1989. This allowed various materials and approaches to be evaluated.
4. Further trials were carried out in Turkey during September 1989.
5. An international resource team was created to field-test and evaluate pilot materials. This team is now involved in the dissemination of the project materials.

The ideas presented in this guidebook have arisen as a result of all these activities. They are, therefore, the product of a remarkable exercise in international collaboration, involving colleagues from many countries and cultures. It is also important to note that these ideas are not complete. Rather they represent a stage of development in a project that is still continuing.

Over the last ten years the numbers of teams around the world that have adopted the UNESCO Resource Pack as part of their teacher education activities have continued to grow. As they do so, they are involved in further research that will contribute to the refinement and expansion of the ideas included in this book. In the same way we hope that readers will see this book not as a blueprint to be followed rigidly, but rather as a source of inspiration that will encourage creativity and innovation.

OVERVIEW OF THE GUIDEBOOK

Chapters 1 and 2 provide accounts of the thinking that informs the approaches recommended in this book. Chapter 1 argues that the dominant approach to educational difficulty can work to the disadvantage of the children it sets out to serve. Consequently an alternative perspective is presented. This perspective sees educational difficulties more positively as indicators of the need for overall school improvement. It also requires a reconsideration of the role and style of teacher education. The nature of the teacher education changes that are necessary are described in Chapter 2.

The next two chapters tell the story of the UNESCO project in detail, including an account of the research undertaken. Chapter 3 describes the processes used to develop and field-test the project materials. Chapter 4 provides an introduction to the materials in the Resource Pack.

The final five chapters provide advice on teacher education approaches. Chapter 5 includes specific suggestions on approaches that seem to be effective in helping teachers to develop their thinking and practice. In Chapters 6, 7 and 8 we provide accounts of teacher education initiatives based upon the UNESCO Resource Pack. Finally, Chapter 9 offers suggestions on setting up and supporting teacher development projects at both the pre-service and in-service stages.

Chapter 1

Rethinking Special Needs

The conceptualization of the special needs task adopted within the UNESCO project 'Special Needs in the Classroom' emerged as a result of a critique of existing approaches and through the processes of collaborative planning and inquiry. This led us to take the view that the dominant perspective on special needs in education works to the disadvantage of the children it is intended to serve. Furthermore, it can be argued that the domination of this thinking on practice in the field has the effect of preventing overall improvements in schooling for all pupils. This chapter examines these arguments in some detail.

THE INDIVIDUAL VIEW

The dominant perspective that guides the organization of responses to children who experience difficulties in school has been characterized as an 'individual gaze' (Fulcher 1989). Put simply this involves constructing or interpreting problems without reference to the wider environmental, social and political contexts in which they occur. Within the UNESCO Resource Pack we refer to this as 'the individual pupil view', within which educational difficulties are defined in terms of pupil characteristics.

This individualized perspective on educational difficulties arises, in part at least, from certain assumptions about the purposes of schooling, the nature of knowledge and the process of learning. In their most extreme form, these assumptions lead to a view of schooling as a process by which those who know (the teachers) are employed to transmit their knowledge to those who need to know (the pupils). With this in mind, schools are organized in ways that will facilitate this transmission process efficiently and are, therefore, assumed to be rational (Skrtic 1991). Consequently, pupils who are perceived as being unable or, indeed, unwilling to take reasonable advantage of the opportunities that are provided are taken to be in some way deficient: the focus is on them as individuals and those of their attributes that would seem to be preventing their progress.

Over the years many approaches have been used to provide help to children experiencing difficulties in school. Differences exist with respect to how their difficulties are defined, the forms of treatment that should be used and the organizational formats that are preferred in order to provide additional help. Whatever the style, however, the dominant perspective is usually individualized, thus requiring a process of identification and assessment based upon a scrutiny of those attributes that are assumed to be interfering with the individual child's learning.

Why, then, do we suggest that this individualized perspective works to the disadvantage of the pupils it is intended to help? Surely a focus on the problems of individual pupils is a basis for positive actions that can help overcome their difficulties. The case rests on the following five sets of arguments:

1. The impact of labels
2. The framing of responses
3. Limitations of opportunity
4. The use of resources
5. The maintenance of the status quo.

Let us consider each of these in turn:

1. The impact of labels

The use of labels to describe individual pupils and summarize the nature of their educational difficulties has been widely critiqued in recent years (Ainscow and Tweddle 1988; Tomlinson 1982). Consequently many teachers are aware of the way in which the process of labelling can lead to a lowering of the expectations they have of certain pupils. In some countries legislation attempts to eliminate the risks associated with labels by abolishing the use of special education categories as the basis of decision-making. However, there is considerable evidence that the phenomenon of labelling continues to have a strong influence on thinking and practice (Fulcher 1989). It may well be that it is the domination of the individualized perspective that most of all encourages labelling in that it encourages teachers to characterize particular pupils in terms of selected attributes assumed to be inhibiting their learning. If this is so, it is necessary to find ways of widening this perspective in order to alleviate the problem.

2. The framing of responses

The second set of arguments with respect to the individualized perspective are to do with the way in which it influences the style of teaching responses that are provided. Focusing attention on particular children in an individualized way leads the school population to be divided into 'types' of children to be taught in different ways or even by different types of teachers. Furthermore, since certain pupils are perceived as being special, it seems common sense that they must require special forms of teaching. I have to say that during my career I have spent considerable time and energy attempting to find special ways of teaching that will help special children to learn successfully (Ainscow and Tweddle 1979). My conclusion now is that no such specialized approaches are worthy of consideration. Whilst certain techniques can help particular children gain access to the process of schooling, these are not in themselves the means by which they will experience educational success. Furthermore, framing our responses in this way tends to distract attention away from much more important questions related to how schooling can be improved in order to help all children to learn successfully.

3. Limitations of opportunity

The third set of arguments about the influence of the individualized perspective is to do with limitations of opportunity. As a result of focusing on selected attributes of individual pupils, it is usual to provide some form of individualized intervention. This may include the presentation of tasks or materials designed on the basis of an analysis of the child's existing attainment; or it may involve additional adult help in order to facilitate their progress. Despite the potential value of these responses on some occasions, we need to recognize that they can also lead to situations in which pupils spend much of the school day working alone. If this is so, it is surely to their disadvantage. Most of us learn most successfully when we are engaged in activities with other people. Apart from the intellectual stimulation that this can provide, there is also the confidence that comes from having other people to provide support and help as we work. If children said to have special needs are working alone for much of their time in school, none of these benefits can accrue.

It is worth adding that the presence of additional adults in a mainstream classroom to provide support for individual pupils can also limit opportunities. Too often the support teacher or classroom assistant becomes a barrier to integration, standing between a particular child and the rest of the class, rather than acting as a facilitator of learning opportunities. If, however, additional adults are seen as a means of increasing the flexibility of the teaching provided for all pupils, it is likely that educational difficulties will be reduced.

4. The use of resources

Issues to do with the use of resources constitute the fourth area of concern with respect to defining educational difficulties using an individualized perspective. Defining educational difficulty in terms of the attributes of individual pupils and conceptualizing responses in terms of specialized teaching lead to an assumption that responses to special needs are dependent upon the provision of additional resources. Resources are undoubtedly important and schools in most countries, even in the developed world, would benefit from better buildings, more equipment and books, smaller classes and more skilful teachers with higher morale. However, attaching additional resources to specific children has a number of potential disadvantages. First of all, it can discourage effort and confidence among teachers, since there is an implication that certain pupils cannot be taught within existing resources. Second, it encourages a waste of time and energy in fighting battles for such resources, including the necessity for additional administrators to manage allocations. Third, there is increasing evidence from around the world that struggles to win additional resources for particular pupils lead to an increase in the proportion of children placed in categories of exclusion (e.g. Crawford 1990; Fulcher 1989; Slee 1991; Wang 1991). Finally, it is worth considering the source of additional resources. Often they are diverted from the general school budget. If this is the case, a ludicrous procedure is taking place by which the 'victims' of a school system are given extra help by transferring finance in such a way that it becomes likely that even more victims will be created.

5. The maintenance of the status quo

The final set of arguments with respect to the individualized perspective is to do with its role in the maintenance of the status quo within a school. It is here that I wish to argue the case that this perspective not only works to the disadvantage of particular pupils but also acts as a barrier to overall school improvement. The dominant approach to the special needs task assumes that the problem is the child's; as a result it excludes from consideration other factors that lie in larger social, political and organizational processes that are external to the individual (Skrtic 1991). Consequently, the organization and curriculum of schools remain largely unquestioned and are assumed to be appropriate for the majority of pupils. In this way opportunities for improvement are missed.

THE CURRICULUM VIEW

Based on these five sets of arguments, the UNESCO project 'Special Needs in the Classroom' has conceptualized the special needs task in a different way. Within the Resource Pack materials this is referred to as 'the curriculum view' and educational difficulties are defined in terms of tasks, activities and classroom conditions.

This wider perspective involves a recognition that individuals have to be viewed within a given context – the progress of individual pupils can be understood only in respect to particular circumstances, tasks and sets of relationships. Furthermore, we have to remember that our understanding of individuals is limited by our own personal resources and previous experience. We can, however, compensate for these limitations by considering the points of view of others who bring additional resources and experience that can help to supplement this understanding.

This wider perspective, therefore, involves teachers becoming more skilled in interpreting events and circumstances, and using the resources of other people around them as a source of support. Its focus is on the improvement of learning conditions as a result of a consideration of difficulties experienced by certain pupils in their classes. In this way, pupils who experience difficulties can be seen more positively as a source of feedback on existing classroom conditions, providing insights as to how these conditions can be improved. Furthermore, given the interconnections between individuals within a given context, it seems reasonable to assume that these improvements are likely to be to the advantage of others in the class. Thus a widening perspective with respect to educational difficulty can be seen as a way of improving schooling for all. In other words, an emphasis on equity is a means of achieving excellence (Skrtic 1991).

IMPROVING SCHOOLS

The perspective on educational difficulties we are recommending means, therefore, that the special needs task is reconstructed as school improvement. What then are the features of such an approach and how might it be achieved?

The now extensive research on effective schools and teaching provides a useful source of ideas as to the sorts of features we should be seeking. For example, Edmonds (1982) has noted the following features that seem to be characteristic of exceptional schools:

1. The principal's leadership and attention to the quality of instruction.
2. A pervasive and broadly understood instructional focus.
3. An orderly, safe climate conducive to teaching and learning.
4. Teacher behaviour that conveys the expectation that all students are expected to obtain at least minimum mastery.
5. The use of measures of pupil achievement as the basis for programme evaluation.

These rather general features have been confirmed by an impressive range of other studies. They are perhaps summed up by Rutter *et al.* (1979) who, when commenting on what makes good schools good, noted that it is:

> Schools which set good standards, where the teachers provide good models of behaviour, where they [the pupils] are praised and given responsibility, where general conditions are good and where the lessons are well-conducted. (p. 178)

It is interesting to compare these findings from research about effective schools with work arising from an earlier project to develop special needs practice in mainstream schools (Ainscow and Muncey 1989) in which it was found that the following features seemed to be common to those schools experiencing success within the project:

1. Effective leadership from a headteacher who is committed to meeting the needs of all pupils.
2. Confidence amongst staff that they can deal with children's individual needs.
3. A sense of optimism that all pupils can succeed.
4. Arrangements for supporting individual members of staff.
5. A commitment to provide a broad and balanced range of curriculum experiences for all children.
6. Systematic procedures for monitoring and reviewing progress.

The common strands between these findings and those from the general literature on effective schools provide further justification for the orientation which we are seeking to encourage. The features of schools said to be effective in meeting special needs are, in fact, the features of effective schools in general.

Moving on from effective schooling to effective teaching, there again seems to be a general consensus of findings within the research literature. A useful synthesis of the findings of this research is provided by Porter and Brophy (1988). They suggest that this provides a picture of effective teachers as semiautonomous professionals who:

- are clear about their instructional goals;
- are knowledgeable about their content and the strategies for teaching it;
- communicate to their students what is expected of them – and why;
- make expert use of existing instructional materials in order to devote more time to practices that enrich and clarify the content;
- are knowledgeable about their students, adapting instruction to their needs and anticipating misconceptions in their existing knowledge;
- teach students metacognitive strategies and give them opportunities to master them;
- address higher – as well as lower – level cognitive objectives;
- monitor students' understanding by offering regular appropriate feedback;

- integrate their instruction with that in other subject areas;
- accept responsibility for student outcomes;
- are thoughtful and reflective about their practice.

Once again, it is interesting to compare these findings with those of Ainscow and Muncey (1989) whose concern, it will be recalled, was with policies for meeting special needs in ordinary schools. Within this study it was found that the most effective teachers:

- emphasize the importance of meaning;
- set tasks that are realistic and challenging;
- ensure that there is progression in children's work;
- provide a variety of learning experiences;
- give pupils opportunities to choose;
- have high expectations;
- create a positive atmosphere;
- provide a consistent approach;
- recognize the efforts and achievements of their pupils;
- organize resources to facilitate learning;
- encourage pupils to work co-operatively;
- monitor progress and provide regular feedback.

The evidence seems to support the view that teachers said to be successful in meeting special needs are to a large extent using strategies that help all pupils to experience success. Indeed we are probably referring to the very same teachers. Thus my argument is that what is now needed is not attempts to define special teaching methods for special children, but effective teaching and learning for all children. As Stoll (1991) argues, 'in an effective school with quality classroom instruction, all children, irrespective of social class differences, can make more progress than all children in an ineffective school with poor teaching methods'.

Examining the research findings summarized so far seems to imply that improvements in teaching and learning are relatively straightforward. If we know broadly what good schools and effective teachers are like, doesn't this provide a recipe for improvement? However, schools and classrooms are complex environments involving a range of unpredictable interacting factors. Consequently bringing about improvements is itself a complex and at times frustrating business.

As we know, change, particularly when it involves people in adopting new ways of thinking and behaving, is difficult and time-consuming. Fullan (1982) argues that for it to be achieved successfully, change has to be understood and accepted by those involved. Understanding and acceptance take time and need encouragement. These problems are made even more complex in educational contexts by what Iano (1986) refers to as 'the inarticulate component of practice'. In other words, the practical knowledge that is acquired only through practice and contact with other practitioners. It is developments in this knowledge that form the basis of improvements in classroom practice.

STAFF DEVELOPMENT

If I reflect upon the most successful school improvement initiatives I have been involved in, they seem to share a strong element of staff development (Ainscow 1991). In this context I am using the term 'staff development' to include a range of processes and activities by which teachers can be helped and help one another to develop their practice.

Looking back at my own experience, I note a number of common features of those initiatives where staff development has had positive effects on the practice of teachers and the progress of pupils, including those said to have special needs. These are:

1. The emphasis has been on developments in the context of particular schools and including classroom-based staff-development activities.
2. They have been conducted in ways that have encouraged collaboration between colleagues.
3. At various stages particular individuals adopted key roles of leadership and co-ordination.
4. Timing was important in the sense that changes in practice always seem to take longer than anticipated.
5. Continued support for individuals is crucial as they wrestle with new ideas and attempt to develop their classroom practice.

In other words, the evidence from my experience is that staff development can facilitate improvements in schooling for all pupils but only when it begins to intrude into the deeper culture of a particular school.

In a very helpful paper Fullan (1990) recently examined the role of staff development as it relates to innovation and institutional development. He suggests that staff development can be seen in one of three ways: as a strategy for the implementation of innovations, as an innovation in its own right or as institutional development.

He concludes that whilst the first two perspectives are useful for certain limited purposes, only the third approach has the potential to make continuing staff development and improvement a way of life in a school. It is through this third perspective that true collaborative cultures of the sort that will help teachers to respond positively to pupil diversity can be achieved.

The proposals we are making, therefore, are intended to create a culture within mainstream schools that will enable them to be more flexible in responding to all children in the community. Such a culture would encourage teachers to see pupils experiencing difficulties not as a problem, but as a source of understanding as to how their practice could be developed.

There is growing recognition that this kind of approach is only likely to occur in contexts where there exists a respect for individuality (Eisner 1990), and, critically, within a culture of collaboration that encourages and supports problem-solving (Fullan 1991; Joyce et al. 1991; Thousand and Villa 1991; Skrtic 1991a). A striking and relevant example of the importance of collaboration is provided by Rosenholtz (1989). Her study of seventy-eight schools indicates that in those where there is a shared consensus, teachers are much more likely to incorporate new ways of responding to their pupils. In such schools teachers seem more willing to persevere, to define 'problem pupils' as a challenge and to actually foster pupil progress. This research leads Rosenholtz to conclude that 'teachers' optimism and enthusiasm are tractable virtues by which students grow, and schools can either strengthen or weaken them through the contextual design of teachers 'work' (p. 138).

SCHOOLS AS PROBLEM-SOLVING ORGANIZATIONS

Assuming that problems and problem-solving are a central part of the process of education, surely schools should be placed where teachers and pupils engage in activities that help them to become more successful at understanding and dealing with the problems they meet. In this sense, problems that occur in schools can be seen as opportunities for learning.

Consequently a necessary strategy in seeking to make schools more responsive to the needs of all children is to find ways of gearing them to problem-solving. In other words schools have to be organizations within which everybody is engaged co-operatively in the task of learning, both pupils and teachers.

Unfortunately, too often schools seem to inhibit co-operation and problem-solving. For example, Gitlin (1987) has investigated the impact of organizational and curriculum structures on the work of teachers. His view is that 'common school structures encourage a teacher that emphasizes management and technical skills, isolate teachers from one another, and "disconnects" them from their students'. Skrtic (1987) characterizes schools as professional bureaucracies that are unsuited to the creation of divergent thinking. Such organizations tend to use what Mintzberg (1979) has called 'pigeonholing', a process by which problems that occur are matched to one of a series of existing standard responses. Mintzberg suggests that a common problem associated with pigeonholing is that 'the professional confuses the needs of his clients with the skills he has to offer them'.

If we are to find ways of encouraging collaborative problem-solving, we need to be sensitive to the nature of schools as organizations. Most of all we have to remind ourselves that schools are not simply buildings, timetables and curriculum plans. First and foremost they are relationships and interactions between people. Consequently, a successful school is one in which the relationships and interactions are facilitated and co-ordinated in order that the people involved can achieve their common mission. Commenting on effective schools and school change, Skrtic (1988) argues that 'at bottom, the difference is people. People acting on their values and affecting what the organization can be'. Or, as Clark, Lotta and Astuto (1984) suggest, 'The search for excellence in schools is the search for excellence in people'.

Why, then, is the idea of groups of people working collaboratively to solve problems and achieve a common mission so difficult to achieve in schools? The work of Karl Weick (1976; 1985) may help to make sense of this issue. He suggests that schools are 'loosely coupled systems' unlike successful business organizations that tend to be more tightly coupled. The loose coupling within schools occurs because they consist of units, processes, actions and individuals tending to operate in isolation from one another. It is encouraged by the goal ambiguity that characterizes schooling. Despite the rhetoric of curriculum aims and objectives, schools consist of groups of people who may have very different values and, indeed, beliefs about the purposes of schooling. To illustrate this point Weick uses the metaphor of a soccer game in which players enter and leave the game at will, and attempt to kick the ball towards several goals that are scattered haphazardly around a circular pitch.

Johnson and Johnson (1989) suggest that schools can be structured in one of three ways: individualistically, competitively or co-operatively. In schools with an individualistic form of organization teachers work alone to achieve goals unrelated to the goals of their colleagues. Consequently there is no sense of common purpose, little sharing of expertise and limited support for individuals. Furthermore such schools often move towards a more competitive form of organization.

In a competitive system, teachers strive to do better than their colleagues, recognizing that their fate is negatively linked. The career progress of one teacher is likely to be enhanced by the failure of others within the school. In this win-lose struggle to succeed, it is almost inevitable that individuals will celebrate the difficulties experienced by their colleagues since these are likely to increase their own chance of success.

Clearly the organizational approach we need to encourage is one that emphasizes co-operation. The aim should be to create a more tightly coupled system. In such a school staff strive for mutual benefit recognizing that they all share a common purpose and, indeed, a common fate. Individuals know that their performance can be influenced positively by the performance of others. This being the case, individuals feel proud when a colleague succeeds and is recognized for professional competence. As Johnson and Johnson argue, 'A clear co-operative structure is the first pre-requisite of an effective school'. A school based upon a co-operative structure is likely to make good use of the expertise of all its personnel, provide sources of stimulation and enrichment that will foster their professional development, and encourage positive attitudes to the introduction of new ways of working. In short, it provides the culture necessary for helping teachers to take responsibility for the learning of all their pupils.

Having said this, a word of warning is necessary. Establishing a culture of co-operation within a school is not a simple matter, not least because it is necessary to do so within a format which does not reduce 'teacher discretion' (Skrtic 1988). Teaching is a complex activity and, consequently, individual teachers must have sufficient autonomy to make flexible decisions that take account of the individual needs of their pupils and the uniqueness of every encounter that occurs. Hence the aim must be a more tightly coupled system, without losing the benefits accruing to loose coupling (West and Ainscow 1991).

REFLECTIVE PRACTICE

One of the key outcomes of schools organized to provide stimulation and support for teachers in order that they can collaborate in problem-solving is that teachers are encouraged to adopt a reflective attitude towards their own practice; teachers are encouraged to learn from experience and experiment with new ways of working alongside and with their pupils and colleagues.

This approach to the development of professional practice represents a very different orientation from the traditional pattern of teacher education. Traditionally teacher education, particularly in the special needs field, has been seen as a search for solutions to solve a technical task (Iano 1986). Consequently, teachers attend courses and workshops to learn about theories and techniques derived from research in order that they can then use these to deal with the perceived problems of individual pupils.

The emphasis within this orientation is on the use of the findings of experimental research studies. Typically these involve the study of the relationship between sets of variables with a view to making generalizations that can be applied across settings. (Harre 1981; House, Lapan and Mathison 1989). Research might, for example, consider the impact of teachers' use of praise upon the social conduct of pupils in order to demonstrate relationships between the two variables, praise and social conduct, so as to prove the existence of laws that would apply in the classrooms of all teachers.

Such investigations are based upon a number of assumptions that are matters of dispute. In particular, they assume that variables such as praise and social conduct can be defined in ways that could be said to apply across settings, times and people. The problems with this are that classrooms are complex environments, and interactions between teachers and pupils are unique, so that the idea of such generalized interpretations are always subject to doubt (Bassey 1990).

When special education was framed as a series of technical tasks concerned with finding solutions to the problems of individual children, this approach to the improvement of practice seemed to provide a reasonable fit. Although issues of research methodology, not least to do with rigour, continued to encourage argument, the idea of seeking to establish laws of cause and effect that could be used to make generalizations about classroom life seemed appropriate.

However, a wider perspective on educational difficulties points to the need for a very different approach to the improvement of practice. Our concern is to find approaches that encourage teachers to learn from their own experience, taking note of evidence from elsewhere certainly, but recognizing the importance of the inarticulate component of practice that is developed through a more intuitive form of learning. Consequently, we want teachers to analyse and reflect upon their own classrooms. Their concern should be with all children in their classes as they interact with particular tasks and processes. The idea of establishing research-based predictions across people, time and contexts is, to say the least, inappropriate.

What is needed is for each teacher to seek deeper understandings of the nature and outcomes of particular educational events and situations. In this sense, the reality of classroom encounters is seen as something that is created in the minds of the people involved rather than something that can be defined objectively, observed systematically and measured accurately (Lincoln and Guba 1985).

In the light of this argument, we wish to promote forms of teacher education that encourage teachers to take responsibility for their own professional learning. Such approaches, as well as having a resonance with teaching as an activity, are also a means of helping teachers to recognize and respond to the wider pressures within which they have to operate. As Heron (1981) suggests, 'persons, as autonomous beings, have a moral right to participate in decisions that claim to generate knowledge about them. Such a right ... protects them ... from being managed and manipulated'.

IMPLICATIONS

Proposing this wider curriculum perspective has major implications for the way in which schools and teachers respond to youngsters experiencing difficulties in learning. It requires four conditions: assessment and recording focused on the interactions between children and teachers in the normal classroom environment; information collected on a continuous basis; a key role for students in reflecting upon their own learning; and improving the quality of teaching and learning provided for *all* pupils as the overall aim. In this context learning difficulties can be seen positively as a source of insight as to how schooling can be improved.

The successful adoption of this perspective requires the involvement of *all* teachers within a school. It is a radical change from the tradition that has reinforced the idea that children with special needs are the responsibility of specialists. Consequently, care must be taken as we attempt to introduce these changes to colleagues who are already hard pressed.

The roles adopted by those perceived as being special needs specialists is vital. Increasingly they must focus on working in ways that encourage the collaborative problem-solving perspective that is central to the proposals made throughout this chapter. It is through the successes of school-based initiatives based on this perspective that attitudes and practices will be developed.

The rest of this book is dedicated to examining ways in which trainee and experienced teachers can be helped to adopt a curriculum view of educational difficulties. It means that the task of special needs is reconstructed as a process of school improvement. Furthermore, teacher development is central to this process.

Chapter 2

School Improvement Through Teacher Development

In the light of our rethinking of the special needs task, how can teachers be helped to adopt a wider perspective to educational difficulties? What approaches to teacher education can contribute to this shift in perspective? These are the issues that are being addressed in the 'Special Needs in the Classroom' project. The responses that I will provide to these questions represent our latest thinking. This may well change, of course, as our work proceeds. In the meantime, the outcomes of the project so far provide some useful pointers to colleagues involved in similar initiatives. Furthermore, they lead to a series of suggestions that may help more generally in the reform of teacher education.

TEACHER DEVELOPMENT

The term 'teacher development' has been adopted rather than the more familiar term 'in-service training' deliberately. Here I am once again attempting to avoid the mistake of using an individualized perspective, in this case with respect to the learning of teachers. So, in a real sense, I am attempting to conceptualize an approach to teacher development that is analogous to the one I have outlined in connection with children's learning. Just as successful classrooms provide the conditions that support and encourage all children's learning, so a successful approach to teacher development must address contextual matters in order to create the conditions that facilitate the learning of adults.

The research evidence available on the effectiveness of teacher-development initiatives is far from encouraging. Despite all the effort and resources that have been utilized, the impact of such programmes in terms of improvements in teaching and better learning outcomes for pupils is rather disappointing (Fullan 1991; Joyce and Showers 1988). What is the explanation for this sad state of affairs? What is the nature of the mistakes that have been made?

As a result of his review of available research evidence, Michael Fullan provides the following summary of the reasons for the failure of in-service education:

1. One-shot workshops are widespread but are ineffective.
2. Topics are frequently selected by people other than those for whom the in-service is provided.
3. Follow-up support for ideas and practices introduced during in-service programmes occurs in only a very small minority of cases.
4. Follow-up evaluation occurs infrequently.
5. In-service programmes rarely address the individual needs and concerns of participants.
6. The majority of programmes involve teachers from many different schools and/or school districts, but there is no recognition of the differential impact of positive and negative factors within the system to which they must return.
7. There is a profound lack of any conceptual basis in the planning and implementation of in-service programmes that would ensure their effectiveness (Fullan 1991, p. 316).

Thus from this analysis we have a picture of in-service initiatives that are poorly conceptualized, insensitive to the concerns of individual participants and, perhaps critically, make little effort to help participants relate their learning experiences to their usual workplace conditions.

A RATIONALE

Extensive use was made of evaluative and research evidence from other similar initiatives, and a wider theoretical literature, to critique the developing rationale of the UNESCO pack. This led to a rejection of the functionalist assumptions that have dominated thinking and practice in special education, and guided much of the work that has gone into teacher development (Skrtic 1991a). The work of the project was influenced by an alternative perspective which offers a very different way of considering human behaviour. This perspective, sometimes referred to as a constructivist or constructionist view, assumes that our perceptions, appreciations and beliefs are rooted in worlds of our own making that we come to regard as reality (Goodman 1978). Consequently, initiatives that operate on the basis of this perspective, described by some as a 'new paradigm' (Heshusius 1989; Iano 1986; Lincoln and Guba 1985; Reason 1988), emphasize the following assumptions:

1. Human behaviour can only be understood with respect to particular contexts.
2. This understanding can only be achieved by a consideration of these contexts as 'wholes'.
3. Events that occur within a given context are assumed to be constructed in the minds of participants and can, therefore, only be understood by taking account of these multiple realities.

The constructivist perspective – and its associated assumptions – have been influential in the development of the project, including its approach to special needs, teacher development, dissemination and evaluation (Ainscow 1993). It has become the guiding theory that has been used with some success to construct an initiative that can be relevant across diverse contexts and cultures. However, as will be seen, it is a perspective that challenges many existing practices in schools and in teacher education and consequently must be adopted with care.

In particular, it is important to recognize that reconstructing the special needs task in terms of school improvement and teacher development is likely to lead to a challenge to the status quo of schooling and teacher education. At a political level it addresses questions to those who create and administer policy; and at a professional level it presents challenges to individual teachers and those involved in their education. Specifically, it requires many to suspend their existing beliefs and assumptions about the origins and nature of educational difficulties in order to consider alternative perspectives. Instead of the traditional search for specialist techniques that can be used to ameliorate the learning difficulties of individuals pupils, the focus must be on finding ways of creating the conditions that will facilitate and support the learning of all children.

These changes of perspectives are not easy to achieve. Teaching is a demanding and intensive activity leaving little time for reflection. Furthermore, the perspectives of teachers are often deeply rooted, having been established through the process of professionalization that occurs during initial training and, perhaps even more significantly, within the workplace (Rozenholtz 1989). This is why the UNESCO project materials seek to influence teacher educators and others involved in the training and further professional development of teachers.

A critical aspect of the change in perspective required relates to the way teachers and others in education conceptualize educational difficulty. In other words, as Schon (1987) suggests, the ways in which problems are 'named and framed'. He notes:

> Through complementary acts of naming and framing, the practitioner selects things for attention and organises them, guided by an appreciation of the situation that gives it coherence and sets a direction for action. (p. 4)

This is, in effect, the constructivist notion of 'world making', as defined by Nelson Goodman (1978).

The aim of these changes is to help teachers and teacher educators to break out of what Fulcher (1989) refers to as the 'individualistic gaze'. This approach to naming and framing the problems experienced by pupils and teachers takes little or no notice of the wider environmental, social and political contexts in which they occur. By focusing attention on particular pupils in this individualized way, it leads the school population to be divided into 'types' of children to be taught in different ways or even by different types of teachers. This has the effect of deflecting attention away from the central issue of how schooling can accommodate pupil diversity. It does this by characterizing special needs as a technical task requiring the provision of special techniques, personnel and physical resources. Within this individualistic gaze, the teacher-education task with respect to special needs is seen as being concerned with introducing teachers to approaches that can be used to ameliorate the problems of individual pupils. Furthermore, the responses that result are often very limiting in that they underestimate the importance of social interactions as a means of facilitating learning (Ainscow and Tweddle 1988).

In encouraging teachers to consider alternative perspectives, however, we are asking them to see pupils experiencing difficulties in their learning as a source of understanding as to how teaching and classroom conditions can be improved. These improvements, it should be recalled, are seen as being to the advantage of all pupils.

In developing the rationale for the materials and approaches recommended in the Resource Pack, the work of Donald Schon (1983; 1987) concerning professional development has been particularly important and helpful. Schon stresses the importance of what he calls 'professional artistry' as a basis for the improvement of practice.

His analysis leads him to be highly critical of existing approaches to professional development in a number of fields, including that of teacher education. The central problem, he argues, lies in the doctrine of technical rationality that dominates thinking within the professions. Embedded in technical rationality is the assumption that a profession is an occupational group whose practice is grounded in knowledge derived from scientific research. As a result, professional competence is seen as the skilful application of theoretical knowledge to the instrumental problems of practice. Within such a view of practice, artistry has little place.

Schon argues that such a view of professional knowledge and practice is inadequate in a number of ways. In terms of our concern here specifically, he suggests that although technical rationality portrays professional competence as a technical problem-solving competence, the problems of the real world do not present themselves as given. Rather they are messy, indeterminate and problematic situations that often arise because of conflicting values. Such problems cannot be resolved by the use of techniques derived from theoretical research but rather call for what Schon calls 'artful competence'. This is a process of clarification of a problematic situation that enables practitioners to redefine their problems in terms of both the ends to be achieved and the means for their achievement.

As a result of his analysis Schon argues that the technical rational model should be replaced by an emphasis on what he calls 'reflecting enquiry'. This leads him to seek approaches to professional development that encourage practitioners to reflect upon taken-for-granted knowledge that is implicit in their actions.

Within the UNESCO project we have been exploring approaches that are informed by Schon's arguments. The traditional, individualistic perspective in special needs work can be seen as an example of the technical rational model with all its limitations and disadvantages (Iano 1986). In seeking ways of working that are based upon reflective inquiry, therefore, we are attempting to overcome the domination of this perspective. Our hope is that by helping teachers to become confident of their own abilities to learn from their experience we can help them to break out of the individualized gaze.

In addition to reflective inquiry, our other area of emphasis is on social processes as a means of facilitating professional development and learning. As we have already seen, effective schools seem to be characterized by a culture of *collaboration* leading to a shared consensus. Whilst our project does not always operate at the whole school level, it does emphasize the importance of collaboration at all levels of the school system as a means of facilitating problem-solving and learning. In this respect we have accepted the argument of Handy and Aitkin (1986):

> Groups allow individuals to reach beyond themselves, to be part of something that none of them would have attained on their own and to discover ways of working with others to mutual benefit. (p. 108)

In summary, then, the 'Special Needs in the Classroom' project attempts to help teacher educators and teachers to become more confident and skilful in developing their own practice by encouraging them to use the resources of others around them (including their pupils) to stimulate their reflections upon difficulties that arise in their classrooms. It is anticipated that where this approach is successful it will lead teachers to become more confident about their ability to cater for pupil diversity. In this way the special needs task is reframed as school improvement and teacher development.

THE UNESCO RESOURCE PACK

The Resource Pack contains the following elements:

1. *Study Materials*. These include an extensive range of readings, stimulus sheets and classroom activities for use during course or workshop sessions.
2. *Training Videos*. These include examples of the various recom-

mended approaches in use during courses and film of follow-up activities in schools.

3. *Course Leaders' Guide* (contained in this guidebook). This provides detailed guidance as to how to organize courses and facilitate sessions based on the study materials. A series of case studies describing projects that have been carried out in a number of countries is also included.

It is important to understand that the materials and activities in the pack encourage course leaders to model at the adult level strategies for teaching that take account of and, indeed, make positive use of student diversity. In this way the features of the pack that are seen as facilitating adult learning within course sessions are intended to be used as a basis for working with classes of children in school.

As we have seen, the content of the materials emphasizes two main strategies for helping teachers to consider alternative perspectives to educational difficulty as a means of improving classroom practice. These are:

- *Reflective inquiry*. Influenced by the writings of Donald Schon (1983; 1987), this is an approach to professional development that encourages practitioners to question taken-for-granted knowledge that is implicit in their actions.
- *Collaboration*. Here teachers are encouraged to use the resources of others around them (including colleagues and pupils) to support them as they reflect upon difficulties that arise in their classrooms.

Our attempts to introduce teacher educators and teachers to these two strategies are based upon five sets of approaches that have been developed and refined within the project *active learning* (approaches that encourage participants to engage with opportunities for learning); *negotiation of objectives* (approaches that enable teacher development activities to take account of the concerns and interests of individual participants); *demonstration, practice and feedback* (approaches that model examples of practice, encourage their use in the classroom and incorporate opportunities for supportive feedback); *continuous evaluation* (approaches that encourage enquiry and reflection as ways of reviewing learning); and *support* (approaches that help individuals to take risks).

Together these five sets of approaches are intended to help teachers to be reflective about their practice and support one another in the process of improvement. These approaches also provided the theoretical basis of the successful field-testing of the Resource Pack that occurred in the eight countries described in Chapter 3. I will now consider these approaches in more detail.

Active learning

Teacher development programmes should be devised in ways that encourage those involved to engage actively with resources that can facilitate their learning. Resources might include course activities, other people's ideas and perspectives, and evidence from elsewhere. The important point to note is that these external resources are intended to be used by teachers to consider their own previous experience, their current ways of working and their existing beliefs and assumptions. They can also be used to reflect upon wider issues that impact upon the teacher's work.

The concept 'active', therefore, does not necessarily imply physical engagement in some activity (although this can often be helpful in encouraging active learning). More important, it means that the learner (in this case the teacher) is being required to take responsibility for engaging with certain experiences whilst taking note of alternative perspectives. In so doing it is anticipated that this will help them to relate new ideas to their existing frames of reference.

Traditional approaches to teacher education, with a strong emphasis on lectures as the main teaching mode, tend to discourage participants from being active learners. Rather, they encourage the view that the course leader has the answers to problems faced by participants and that the process of development simply requires the transmission of this knowledge. This creates a sense of dependence between teacher and learner, and implies that the solutions being offered are both relevant and easily transferred to different classrooms. As noted earlier, the evidence indicates that this lack of attention to linking in-service experience is one of the mistakes of much existing practice.

The project explored a range of approaches that seem to encourage active learning. Many of these involve various forms of co-operative group work within which participants engage in problem solving. They encourage participants to recognize the value of considering alternative points of view and the importance of collaboration. They can also help individuals overcome the fear of change. However, these approaches are not easy to use and, therefore, within the project considerable emphasis is placed on developing the skills of group work in those wishing to use the Resource Pack.

Negotiation of objectives

The leader of a course or workshop session faces similar problems to those encountered by teachers in school. In particular there is the issue of how to manage the class as a whole and, at the same time engage the interests and concerns of individual participants. Approaches that attempt to negotiate objectives are an attempt to address this key issue.

Starting from the assumption that participants have agreed to participate in some form of teacher-development process as a result of discussions about the general aims and content, what is needed are procedures that help individuals to determine their own learning objectives within the overall programme and ways by which course leaders can become aware of these objectives. In this way activities can be designed to take account of those concerns and, of course, to utilize the particular interests of individual participants.

Discussion clearly must be a central approach for this process of negotiation. In addition participants may be asked to draw pictures of their classrooms in order to consider aspects of their practice. The process of drawing, whilst initially somewhat unsettling for some participants, enables them to think more analytically about issues in their workplace.

Similarly, the use of writing is a powerful means of helping teachers to define and review aspects of their practice with a view to determining their learning objectives. With this in mind, courses based upon the UNESCO Resource Pack encourage leaders and participants to keep journals in which they write about their classrooms, the experience of the course and the issues that they are trying to address.

Demonstration, practice and feedback

Possibly the most difficult issue facing those who try to work with teachers in developing classroom practice is how to incorporate new ways of working into existing repertoires. Teaching in schools is a very demanding business, leaving little time for experimenting with new approaches – teachers' priorities tend to be to do with managing the classes they are expected to teach. Furthermore, the culture of many schools is highly individualized, providing little or none of the support that might enable and encourage teachers to explore alternative ways of work (Little 1982).

Approaches based upon demonstration, practice and feedback are intended to help create the conditions that will give teachers confidence to take some calculated risks in order to develop their practice. Demonstrations provide opportunities to see alternative classroom approaches in practice; they may simply encourage teachers to reflect once again upon their own ways of working or they may stimulate the trial of a different technique. Demonstration can take a variety of forms. For example, it may mean observing a colleague at work, visits to other schools or the study of video recordings.

Within the UNESCO project further demonstrations of practice are provided by course leaders during the sessions themselves. In this way the teacher educator is expected to demonstrate a commitment to teaching for diversity through the ways in which the sessions are conducted. A powerful feature of this approach, of course, is that participants are at the receiving end of these ways of working and, therefore, have the opportunity to judge the impact upon their own learning.

Alongside demonstrations, the use of practice and feedback is intended to give specific help to participants as they attempt to explore new ways of working. Practice and feedback may be conducted initially in simulated contexts, possibly using the course participants as 'guinea pigs' as alternative teaching approaches are tested. However, it is essential for this to be extended into the teacher's usual workplace to allow a real possibility of continued use of new ways of working. The most helpful approach here is the notion of partnership teaching or, as it is sometimes called, peer coaching (Joyce and Showers 1988). This involves pairs of colleagues working in one another's classrooms as they attempt to review aspects of their practice and experiment with alternative ways of working. This form of partnership is a powerful strategy for developing classroom practice, but it requires a high level of confidence and trust between participants. We have found that it is necessary to agree specific guidelines and ground rules that enable these conditions to be met.

Continuous evaluation

As a further strategy for encouraging teachers to take responsibility for their own learning, it is necessary to encourage processes of continuous evaluation. These involve an emphasis on enquiry and reflection through which teachers collect and review information as they attempt to develop their own thinking and practice.

The learning journals referred to earlier provide one important means of encouraging teachers to inquire into aspects of their work. Within the project once initial reluctance to write in this way was overcome, the use of the journal was adopted with enthusiasm. Indeed, many participants in the field-testing of the Resource Pack reported that writing about their teaching had become an essential feature of their practice.

Within course sessions a variety of structured activities can also be used to encourage evaluation of learning. For example, groups may be asked to summarize their work and give an account to the rest of the course members. Similarly, groups may be asked to present the outcomes of their activities in the form of a poster illustrating their main ideas. The central strategy here involves people helping one another to draw out implications and messages from shared experience in ways that encourage individuals to recognize their own learning.

All these reporting strategies can provide course leaders with further information about the individual perspectives of their participants. They also give feedback on how far activities are catering for the interests of course members and helping them to achieve their objectives.

Support

The approaches to teacher development summarized here can be extremely demanding and, at times, stressful for participants and course leaders. The emphasis placed on inquiry, questioning and the consideration of alternative perspectives cuts across the conventional boundaries between teachers and students. They can expose gaps in understanding and knowledge, areas of prejudice and unthought-out assumptions. The challenge to individuals' perspectives and ways of working can be destabilizing. Consequently, it is essential to establish a strong infrastructure of support that will help participants to take some risks with respect to their thinking and practice. Some of the approaches already described, such as group work and partnership teaching, help to provide a supportive network. In addition, a more supportive atmosphere should be encouraged through the establishment of friendly, warm relationships and an atmosphere of openness between participants and course leaders. This may not always be so easy to achieve, however, particularly within school-based initiatives, where existing differences between teachers may surface during staff development activities.

Experience using the Resource Pack to set up teacher development initiatives suggests that success is more likely if care is taken in planning. The aim must be to ensure appropriate arrangements for the support of the initiative at the following three stages:

1. The *initiation* stage, in order to ensure that all involved are clear about the expectations and commitments that are involved.
2. The *implementation* stage, so that necessary arrangements are made to support all participants and leaders as they engage in development activities.
3. The *follow-up* stage, where it is vital that agreement has been reached to provide support to participants as they explore new ways of working in their own classrooms.

CONCLUSION

In summary, therefore, these five sets of approaches are intended to provide a supportive context for reflective enquiry, resources and experiences that stimulate this approach to teacher development, methods of scrutinizing and recording the outcomes, and help as participants attempt to develop aspects of practice in their classrooms. The project's experience indicates that participation in teacher development initiatives based upon these ideas encourages teacher educators and teachers to widen their perspectives on the nature of educational difficulty and, in so doing, to develop their practice. Detailed suggestions about how to organize course sessions based upon these ideas are provided in Chapter 5.

Chapter 3

Developing the Resource Pack

Following the international consultations and initial trials of materials referred to in the Introduction, a pilot version of the Resource Pack was put together in 1990. Arrangements were then made to carry out trials of these materials with a view to collecting data that could be used to inform the final version of the pack, including a method for its dissemination. A further aim of the field-testing process was to create an international resource team that could be used to support the widening of the work of the project.

In this chapter we describe the process of field-testing and present a general account of the evaluations that were carried out. More detailed accounts of this field-testing are provided in Chapters 6, 7 and 8.

SETTING UP THE FIELD-TESTING

In April 1990 two co-ordinators from each of eight countries took part in a two-week workshop/seminar at the University of Zimbabwe. The group included university lecturers, educational administrators, teachers and one headteacher. The first week took the form of a demonstration workshop during which I used materials from the Resource Pack to conduct a series of course sessions for the co-ordinators and a further group of local teachers and student teachers. In the second week, the demonstrated workshop was evaluated as the basis of a seminar in which the international co-ordinators planned together the ways in which they would field-test the Resource Pack in their own countries.

This field-testing was completed by March 1991 and each team of co-ordinators prepared an evaluation report about their work. The main aim of the field-testing was to gather information that could be used to inform the further development of the Resource Pack and to plan its future dissemination. In this way it has been possible to establish the sixteen co-ordinators into an international resource team, collaborating in the design and promotion of the overall project.

In terms of evaluation, our central question was, 'How can the Resource Pack be developed and disseminated in a way that will be appropriate for teachers in different countries?' With this in mind, the evaluation was based upon a multi-site case study approach (Miles and Huberman 1984) in which individual reports attempted to explain what happened as the resource materials were used in a particular context. In order to be consistent with the constructivist perspective, reports included interpretations of these events from the points of view of *all* participants. The ways in which the materials and ideas related to the social, cultural and educational tradition of each participating country were of particular interest (Miles 1989).

Whilst the emphasis was on providing accounts that made sense of what happened in each national context, comparisons between the experience in different countries were also needed. Consequently, a framework was agreed amongst the team of co-ordinators to ensure a common pattern for evaluation reports. This framework consisted of a series of evaluation questions addressed to course leaders and participants related to five aspects of the field-testing:

> *Implementation* – the use of materials from the Resource Pack within teacher education contexts
> *Process* – interactions based upon the materials associated with the Resource Pack
> *Content* – ideas and approaches presented in the materials
> *Design* – the format of the Resource Pack, including the various written materials
> *Outcomes* – changes of attitude, thinking or practice thought to have occurred as a result of the use of the Resource Pack.

Table 3.1 The evaluation questions

1. Implementation
   1.1 How was the Resource Pack used?
       1.1.1 Who were the participants?
       1.1.2 What was the programme?
       1.1.3 What sections of the pack were used?

      1.1.4 What modifications were made to the materials?

  1.2 What forms of participation occurred?

      1.2.1 What did participants do?

      1.2.2 How far were they engaged in the activities?

      1.2.3 Did any factors have an influence on the involvement of participants?

2. Process

  2.1 What were the reactions of course leaders to the approaches used?

      2.1.1 What approaches were successful?

      2.1.2 What difficulties were experienced?

      2.1.3 What was learned about the approaches used?

  2.2 What were the reactions of participants to the style of the sessions?

      2.2.1 What were the most valuable aspects of the sessions?

      2.2.2 What difficulties were experienced?

      2.2.3 How enjoyable were the sessions?

3. Content

  3.1 What were the reactions of course leaders to the content of the materials, including the Course Leaders' Guide?

      3.1.1 How relevant is the content?

      3.1.2 What important issues are not dealt with?

      3.1.3 How helpful was the Course Leaders' Guide?

  3.2 What were the reactions of participants to the content of the materials?

      3.2.1 What difficulties were experienced in dealing with the ideas presented in the materials?

      3.2.2 How relevant is the content?

      3.2.3 What was the most useful content?

      3.2.4 What important additional issues should be included in the materials?

4. Design

  4.1 What were the reactions of course leaders to the design of the pack?

      4.1.1 Did the format of the pack help in the planning of the course?

      4.1.2 Are there any design features that should be changed?

  4.2 What were the reactions of participants to the design of the materials?

4.2.1 What was the reaction to the layout of the materials?
4.2.2 How appropriate was the language used in the text?
4.2.3 What modifications to the materials might be helpful?

5. Outcomes

5.1 What happened to course leaders as a result of the field-testing?
    5.1.1 Was there any impact upon attitudes and thinking?
    5.1.2 Have there been any changes in practice?
    5.1.3 What local circumstances influenced the outcomes of the field-testing?
5.2 What happened to participants as a result of the course?
    5.2.1 Have there been any changes in attitude and thinking?
    5.2.2 Have there been any changes in practice?
    5.2.3 What local circumstances influenced the outcomes of the course?

The actual evaluation questions are presented in Table 3.1 data that could be used to address the evaluation questions was collected by the following procedures:

1. *Course journal*. This was simply a diary in which co-ordinators and others who acted as course leaders wrote their thoughts, comments and reflections on the running of each course session. It contained two types of information: factual notes about what occurred and interpretative comments. Its content was intended to be helpful in the process of planning course sessions. Afterwards, those who read the evaluation reports were also able to consider the content of the journal in order to have a better understanding of what happened during the field-testing. Where there was more than one leader for a particular course, in most cases they each kept separate journals.

2. *Group reports*. Towards the end of a course and, where appropriate, at key stages within a longer course, participants were asked to work in small groups to prepare written reports. They were given a list of questions and asked to consider which of these seemed to be relevant to their considerations. They were also requested to make comments on any other significant issues that they believed to be important. These reports were written in a form that could be accessible to a wider audience.

3. *Participant questionnaires*. These were completed anonymously by all individual participants after the group reports had been completed. The aim was to provide individuals with an opportunity to give their private views on aspects of the course. It was also intended that the group discussions would be useful in helping participants to formulate their ideas.
4. *Observations*. Where possible, follow-up observations of participants in the classroom were undertaken in order to judge the impact of the course on their practice. In some cases video recordings were made. Video recordings were also made during the course sessions. These were needed by course leaders in order to reflect upon their own practice and were also used as a means of evaluating the level of implementation of project ideas in each of the field-testing sites.

Care was taken in establishing the reliability of findings. In particular, co-ordinators were asked to collaborate with their colleagues, including participants, in order to verify their interpretations. Recording and taking account of multiple perspectives was emphasized throughout the field-testing. Interpretations of the data were also subject to triangulation, a process of using two or more sets of information to study and validate an account of one event (Lincoln and Guba 1985).

In the months following the submission of the evaluation reports, further information was gathered through the exchange of letters with co-ordinators and as a result of meetings and interviews that I was able to have with most of these colleagues. In this way, issues arising from the reports were examined in more detail and plans for the improvement of the Resource Pack agreed.

Some details of the contexts within which the field-testing took place are provided in Table 3.2. In total, the sixteen co-ordinators worked with two hundred and thirty-five participants. As can be seen, the sites involved represented a diversity of national, cultural, linguistic and teacher education contexts. All involved the use of materials from each of the four modules in the Resource Pack in courses or workshops consisting of at least thirty hours of instructional contact. Some of these were intensive (such as one-week workshops), whereas others involved sessions spread over a period of months. Most included opportunities for participants to carry out follow-up activities with pupils in schools.

Table 3.2. Summary of field-testing sites

Canada

(Site 1) Used as part of a school-wide staff development project in a large community school serving a remote community in the north (seventeen participants, plus awareness sessions with forty-five members of staff).

(Site 2) Part of an award-bearing university summer school for experienced teachers (twenty-three participants).

Chile

A course conducted in Spanish for eighteen teachers from regular schools, including fourteen headteachers.

India

(Site 1) An in-service course, in English, for sixteen primary and secondary teachers, including seven special education teachers.

(Site 2) A workshop for twenty-six student teachers in a college, conducted in Hindi.

Jordan

A course for eleven teachers representing one private school and ten teachers from five government schools. Medium of communication, Arabic.

Kenya

Used with sixteen second year students in a teachers college in preparation for and during a period of school practice.

Malta

A workshop for twenty-eight learning support teachers working with underachieving pupils in primary schools.

Spain

A course carried out in Spanish for twenty teachers from ten schools involved in the Government's integration programme, plus seven advisers.

Zimbabwe

A programme for fifteen teacher educators from different colleges and representing different subject areas.

Chapters 6, 7 and 8 provide summary accounts of the field-testing events in each of the eight countries, including an indication of some of the significant lessons that emerged. These accounts are based upon the excellent and detailed reports submitted by each team of co-ordinators.

The evaluation data indicate that in all of the field-testing sites the materials were used as intended and that course leaders worked in ways that were largely consistent with the five sets of approaches outlined in Chapter 2. Inevitably difficulties did arise as co-ordinators attempted to utilize these approaches; an analysis of these problems was very useful in rewriting the materials. In addition, many new ideas and extra materials were developed by members of the resource team and are incorporated in the final Resource Pack.

Some co-ordinators found difficulty in moving away from their previous ways of working, based, as they perhaps were, on a technical/rational perspective. Many reported experiencing considerable strain as a result of the intellectual demands created by teaching approaches based upon active learning and reflective inquiry. In particular, the need to organize and monitor group processes, debrief activities and summarize outcomes are very demanding. Many also referred to problems associated with use of time during course sessions, particularly when these were part of intensive programmes that did not allow sufficient opportunities for course leaders and participants to reflect upon activities that had taken place.

However, all the evaluation reports reflect a sense of acceptance and optimism about the approaches that were used. This was apparent even when co-ordinators were working in very difficult and stressful conditions, not least in Jordan where the field-testing took place during the period just prior to the outbreak of war and in India where there was a certain amount of civil unrest.

Particular contextual factors created difficulties in certain places. For example, a number of co-ordinators reported hostility from certain of their colleagues who, it seems, were unhappy with the emphasis on active learning approaches. Some of the student teachers experienced negative reactions from experienced teachers when they attempted to reorganize classrooms in order to move away from more traditional organizational formats. Difficulties also sometimes arose when the materials were used as part of school-based staff development programmes. Once again negative reactions seemed to occur when approaches were introduced that appeared to challenge existing patterns of working.

The data indicate that the five sets of approaches emphasized in the project were well received and made a significant impact on all of the sites. The use of co-operative group work and the idea of negotiating learning objectives were particularly well regarded. However, there is also a clear indication in many of the reports that the introduction of these ways of working tended to create some negative reactions during early course sessions. For example, a number of the reports note that the participating teachers were not used to taking responsibility for their own learning and showed discomfort when this idea was introduced. All of this can be very stressful for course leaders, leading them to be tempted into reverting to more didactic styles of working.

Some of the co-ordinators also felt a need to offer more practical strategies to their participants, perhaps feeling that the emphasis on reflective inquiry lacked 'hard content'. This tendency has to be resisted, however, particularly if we are to take seriously the view of Donald Schon (1987) when he states:

> the more we integrate in a curriculum the knowledge and skills that students, in our judgement, need to learn, the more we make it difficult for them to function as reflective designers of their own education. (p. 341)

Overall the data seem to indicate a strong feeling that the subject content of the materials in the Resource Pack is relevant to teachers in all of these national contexts. By and large the materials seem to be concerned with topics and issues that are perceived to be real and relevant. One co-ordinator reported that towards the end of the course a participant had been most surprised to hear that the materials had not been written especially for teachers in her own country. Clearly the constructivist approach of using stimulus materials as a means of encouraging participants to draw out ideas from their own experience is an effective strategy for taking account of diversity. In this way, to a large extent, participants are constructing their own content. The opportunity to negotiate individual learning objectives and programmes of activity is also a significant way of catering for individual interests.

Thus it would seem that the Resource Pack has appropriate stimulus materials, focusing on issues that are meaningful and relevant to teachers in different countries, and using activities and processes that enable participants to construct their own agendas for discussion through inquiry, reflection and collaboration. Indeed a participant in Chile remarked:

> 'The course has no content and so enables us to learn how to reflect.'

Similarly, a teacher in Spain noted:

> 'I have learned that if we want to look for and find solutions to our pupils' problems we have to reflect – because the solution is in ourselves.'

A pattern that was noted, however, that needs to be considered, concerns the reactions of those teachers who had previously been exposed to specialized training with respect to special education. Some evidence in the data suggests that members of this group experienced greater difficulty in accepting the value of the approaches used in the Resource Pack. It would seem that their previous experience of techniques reflecting the 'individualized gaze' may act as a barrier when they are asked to consider unusual ways of working. It may also be the case, of course, that they see these alternative approaches as threatening their status as experts in teaching special children, a status that has been given credibility by the widespread acceptance of the doctrine of technical rationality.

OUTCOMES

It is very difficult to measure the outcomes of a project of this sort. Our aspirations are ambitious and evidence of their achievement would require prolonged engagement within the contexts of the various participants, including those of the teachers and the teacher educators. Nevertheless, the indications with respect to both course participants and co-ordinators are, to say the least, very encouraging. In all the reports there is extensive evidence that the activities carried out made a significant impact upon peoples' ideas. As one participant noted: 'I go to bed with the course in mind'.

The data include many interesting anecdotal accounts that provide insights into the ways in which participants reacted to their experiences during courses and workshops. The following example gives a flavour of these accounts. A teacher in Canada wrote about the way in which her participation in a course based upon the Resource Pack had transformed her thinking. She described her unease about being asked to take responsibility for her own learning and how she felt uncharacteristically tongue-tied when asked to participate in group activities. Noting the insecurity that can arise when traditional teaching approaches are absent, she writes:

> 'I began to nostalgically think back to courses past where I could succeed by staying in safe boundaries. I had learned to feel secure when I was told how to think and at peace in a learning environment where I was only required to passively absorb what information I could and reproduce it at well-scheduled intervals.'

She makes reference to the fact that the Chinese character for change is a combination of the characters 'fear' and 'opportunity' (an idea presented in the Resource Pack). She recalls experiencing the fear but was helped through the course activities to take the opportunities for learning. All of this led her to reflect on the issue of pupils with special needs. At the outset of the course there had been little doubt in her mind that the problem was the child's and so it was the child that needed attention. She writes:

> 'The classroom was the mountain, and the child, Mohammed. Of course it made sense that Mohammed was the one to move.'

Through the experience of the course, however, she sensed her assumptions being challenged and her point of view changing. She concludes:

> 'Although individual learning styles influence the rate of a child's development, the learning environment can adapt to the individual if tasks are presented differently, resources teachers provide are varied, and the ways in which the teacher organizes the classroom and its priorities are modified. The mountain can move to Mohammed.'

Many of the participants describe their intention to change their practice in the light of their experiences. Examples of changes are also reported in some detail. This may lead to difficulties since, as we have already noted, such developments may be perceived as challenging existing policies with respect to organization, curriculum and assessment. Attempting to teach in ways that respond to pupil diversity may be seen as a subversive activity. This indicates the need to use the Resource Pack in contexts where extensive negotiations have been undertaken prior to any initiative, in order to clarify expectations and ensure positive support.

Probably the most significant impact of the field-testing has been upon the thinking and practice of the members of the international resource team. In their journals, video recordings and evaluation reports there is ample evidence that all of these co-ordinators have experienced significant rethinking of the theoretical basis of their work. For example, a very experienced teacher educator in Spain describes how the project has altered his perspective on special needs and the role of teacher education. He refers to:

'discovering that both the learning modalities and the learning situations we foster in the children are equally applicable in the training of adults.'

and

'verifying that the best learning source is the analysis of our own experience in a context of support and collaboration among colleagues.'

He therefore concludes:

'in future I will not be able to work with the traditional approach.'

The reactions of the co-ordinators to their experiences and the changes these fostered in their thinking and practice seemed to be entirely positive. The statement made by the members of the resource team in Chile was typical:

'Professionally speaking, as concerns the training activities we have been involved in, we think that the work carried out has been the most gratifying and positive experience we have encountered.'

Continued contact with the resource team following on from the completion of the field-testing suggests that these changes in thinking and practice have been sustained and, indeed, generalized throughout their work. In this respect there is strong evidence from this project confirming findings from elsewhere (for instance Joyce and Showers 1988), that approaches to the professional development of teacher educators that involve demonstrations of method followed by peer collaboration at the stage of implementation of new ways of working are very powerful.

CONCLUSION

In the ten years since the UNESCO Resource Pack was published the materials have been translated into many different languages and used in over eighty countries. The main strategy has been to strengthen existing national projects as a basis for gradual regional development. In this way we have attempted to increase the number of resource people that are able to demonstrate the use of the Resource Pack in different parts of the world.

Major projects based on the Resource Pack have been carried out in countries as diverse as China, Thailand, Ghana, Laos, Italy, Portugal, Romania and Spain. There is also widespread use of the Pack in Latin America, with support from the UNESCO office in Santiago de Chile.

Beyond the specific UNESCO project it is possible to begin drawing out implications for others who wish to help teachers to respond positively to pupil diversity. Specifically we can draw attention to the importance of conceptual clarity when planning such initiatives.

Ture Jonsson makes a distinction between efficiency and effectiveness. Efficiency, he suggests, is to do with 'doing things right'. Effectiveness, on the other hand, is about 'doing the right things'. This distinction helps us to understand some of the mistakes that have occurred in the special needs field. So much of the time and effort that has been used in attempts to develop policies for integration have, in my view, been concerned with matters of efficiency. Regrettably much less attention has been paid to conceptualizing what it is we should be trying to achieve. As a consequence, we have witnessed the development in a number of countries of policies and practice that, despite good intention, seem to work to the disadvantage of the very children they set out to serve. Furthermore, we see the continued expansion of separate provision of various forms, despite the stated aim of achieving integrated schooling.

The central message that has emerged from the work of this project is that those engaged in attempting to foster forms of schooling that are inclusive must pay careful attention to the ways in which they 'name and frame' their activities. Specifically they would be wise to conceptualize their special needs tasks in terms of school improvement (and, quite possibly, school reform) and teacher development. Such perspectives will enable them to recognize the importance of contextual influences on the learning of children and teachers, thus avoiding the limitations of the individualized gaze.

Having said that, it is vital to keep in mind some of the difficulties experienced by course leaders and participants as they attempted to engage with the ideas and perspectives presented through the materials in the Resource Pack. In particular we should note the difficulties experienced by those who had previously been exposed to special education training courses. These difficulties can be explained, at least in part, as arising when individuals attempt to break out of the technical/rational perspective that still dominates so much thinking and practice in education, particularly in the special needs field. As we know this doctrine assumes a belief in science-based professional action. It also ignores conflict by assuming consensus about ends and by attending exclusively to means. In this way it encourages a concern with efficiency rather than effectiveness.

Olson (1989) analyses why, despite mounting criticism, the technical rational orientation persists in education. He comes to the conclusion that this is because of the way it appears to meet the needs of administrators and teachers. Central to his argument is the notion of hazards, a concept he borrows from Goffman (see Olson 1989). Hazards are occasions when reputations are at risk. The great appeal of technical rationality is that it makes decision-making and problem-solving less hazardous, since failures can be blamed on science itself. Olson sums up the argument as follows:

> being able to involve science in support of one's decision off-sets some of the risks of failure since science has to carry some of the blame if things do not go well. (p. 105)

A project of the sort described in this chapter increases the risk of hazard in that it requires those involved to look to themselves and their colleagues in order to find solutions to the problems they face. It also adds further pressure by encouraging participants to work in ways that are very different from existing practice and, in so doing, raise questions that may be perceived as being threatening or even subversive by those around them. It is hardly surprising, therefore, that despite attempts to encourage a supportive environment, there will be times when some will prefer to stay within safer boundaries.

Chapter 4

The Contents of the Resource Pack

As a result of an analysis of the data gathered during the field-testing of the pilot version of the UNESCO Resource Pack, a rationale for the further development of the overall project was put together. While these data were being analyzed, extensive discussions took place between members of the international resource team. These discussions took the following forms:

1. Written communications through letters
2. Meetings held during further workshops and courses led by resource team members.
3. Interviews that I was able to carry out with members of the team.

In the light of all these activities related to the analysis of our findings, we established:

1. A refinement of the approach taken to special needs in education
2. A refinement of the approach taken to teacher development
3. A refinement of the approaches to be used with the Resource Pack
4. Modifications and additions to the contents of the pack
5. Modifications to the design and layout of the pack
6. The development of a plan for the dissemination of the pack

This chapter explains the layout and contents of the pack.

OVERVIEW OF THE RESOURCE PACK

The materials in the Resource Pack are provided in a loose-leaf form. This is a deliberate decision made in order to encourage flexibility in their use. Those using the materials should feel free to modify them to suit the needs of particular contexts. In the same way elements of the pack can be ignored, or additional materials added.

Where such changes are made, however, these decisions should take account of the overall rationale of the pack, as described in this guide-book.

The pack includes the following elements:

MODULES

The materials are arranged in four modules as follows:

Module 1 – An introduction to 'Special Needs in the Classroom'
Module 2 – Special needs: definitions and responses
Module 3 – Towards effective schools for all
Module 4 – Help and support

Individual modules can be used independently of one another or, indeed in any order.

Study Materials

Each module has a set of study materials that provide an overall introduction to the issues to be considered. To help readers to study this material a number of features have been incorporated. These are:

Guides. Introductions that help focus the reader's attention on the topic to be presented.
Points to consider. These questions encourage readers to question the material they have read and relate it to their own experience.
Brief summaries. At the end of the study material a single page summary is provided (Figure 4.1 is an example from Module 2). In some contexts course leaders may feel that these should be used *instead of* the full version. They might also be made into transparencies for use on an overhead projector.

It is anticipated that course participants will have read the study material prior to the sessions that are to deal with the particular module.

Module 2

Summary

Two ways of looking at educational difficulties:

1 The Individual Pupil View
   (i.e. difficulties defined in terms of pupil characteristics)
   Based upon the following ideas:

   • A group of children can be identified who are special

   • These children need special teaching in response to their problems

   • It is best to teach children with similar problems together

   • Other children are normal and benefit from existing teaching

2 The Curriculum View

   (i.e. difficulties defined in terms of tasks, activities and classroom conditions)

   Based upon the following ideas:

   • Any child may experience difficulties in school

   • Such difficulties can point to ways in which teaching can be improved

   • These improvements lead to better learning conditions for all pupils

   • Support should be available as teachers attempt to develop their practice

This course aims to help you to become a better teacher. It is about finding ways of helping all children to learn.

Figure 4.1 Example from Module 2

Units

The units attached to each module provide the basis for course activities. Their purpose is to focus attention on practical implications of the ideas raised in the study materials. The format for the units is as follows:

Instruction sheets. These include the unit aims, explanation of activities and evaluation issues. Usually course participants will be given these sheets in order to encourage them to take an active role in the activities. (Figure 4.2 is an example from Unit 3.4).

Discussion materials. This material provides the basis for course activities (Figure 4.3 is an example from Unit 1.5). Often participants will be asked to study these materials prior to the course session in which they will be discussed. It should be noted that not all units contain discussion materials.

Individual units can be used independently of one another.

Module 3

Unit 3.4 Classroom factors

Unit aim

To consider classroom factors that influence children's learning.

Activities

1 Consider the 'Classroom strategies chart'. This was produced by a group of teachers who included the ways they use to help individual pupils learn in their classrooms. In the empty boxes you can add any other strategies that you find useful.

2 Put a star against the there strategies that you think are most useful to you. Remember, our concern is with strategies that help you respond to individuals in the class.

3 In groups compare you chart with others. Then choose one strategy as a group and work out a plan for using this strategy in the classroom. Try to make use of all the expertise in you working group.

4 Form new groups consisting of one member of each of the previous working groups. Each member presents the findings of his/her working group.

Evaluation issues

1 Has this activity helped you to pinpoint aspects of you teaching that could be improved or developed?

2 Did you find useful to discuss classroom practice with other teachers?

Figure 4.2

Module 1: What do we know about learning?

1 *Learning is never complete*

 Even as adults, our understanding continues to develop as we test our new ideas against previous knowledge. Old ideas can be changed in the light of new experiences.

2 *Learning is individual*

 Even if a whole group of children – or adults – are exposed to the same experience, the learning that takes place will be different for each individual. This is because each individual, child or adult, brings to every situation a unique blend of previous experience.

3 *Learning is a social process*

 Some learning takes place in a group. Sharing learning with others can be stimulating.

4 *Learning can be enjoyable*

 This is something that many adults seriously doubt, when they think back to their own schooling. However, learning can be hard, and enjoyable at the same time. Even making mistakes can be part of the fun – how many times did you fall off when you learned to ride a bike?

5 *Learning is active*

 Someone else can teach us, but no one else can do our learning for us. Learning requires our active engagement, in doing and talking.

6 *Learning means change*

 The Chinese written character for change is a combination of the characters of pain and opportunities. As adults we are responsible for keeping the balance manageable for individual children. For us, too, learning may mean painful changes. Sometimes we need to let go of deeply held convictions. The challenge of change through learning may be experienced as exhilarating or as daunting. Often it is both.

This material is reproduced with permission form:

Drummond, M.J. et al. (1989) *Working with Children: Developing a Curriculum for the Early Years. National Children's Bureau.*

Figure 4.3

Videos

There are three video programmes associated with the Resource Pack. These are as follows:

1. *Introduction to Special Needs in the Classroom*. This ten-minute promotional film is intended to inform people about the project. It might also be used at the beginning of a course or workshop as an introduction.
2. *Inclusive Schools*. This sixty-minute film tells the stories of five schools in different parts of the world that are experiencing some success in responding positively to pupil diversity.
3. *Demonstration Programme*. This is a fifty-minute film illustrating the teacher education approaches used with the Resource Pack. It is intended for training purposes only.

Additional Reading

No additional reading is recommended in the Resource Pack. This decision was taken because of the difficulties of access to books and journals in some parts of the world. It also allows course leaders to recommend additional reading that is particularly relevant to teachers in their own countries.

DETAILS OF THE CONTENTS

The contents of the materials in the Resource Pack are explained in the following pages.

MODULE 1 – AN INTRODUCTION TO 'SPECIAL NEEDS IN THE CLASSROOM'

STUDY MATERIAL 1:

This material provides an introduction to the project, including an account of its development through a process of international collaboration and research. This led to the development of five approaches that make the materials associated with the project relevant to teachers in different countries. Courses and workshops based upon the materials have to be conducted in a flexible way in order to take account of the interests of individual participants. The aim is to encourage participants to take responsibility for their own learning.

UNITS IN MODULE 1:

1.1 *What do you expect?* Participants are expected to determine their own learning objectives within the general aim, of the course. This activity helps individuals to review their expectations.

1.2 *A policy for evaluation.* Continuous evaluation is seen as being a crucial part in the use of these materials. This unit provides some suggestions as to how this evaluation should be undertaken.

1.3 *Learning lessons.* This course is all about learning – children's learning and adult learning. The purpose of this unit is to help participants to think about themselves as learners.

1.4 *Looking at classrooms.* This unit begins the process of encouraging participants to review their own practice as teachers. It also helps in the refinement of learning objectives for the course.

1.5 *Children's learning.* In this unit participants continue thinking about learning. Here the concern is with the learning of children.

1.6 *School-based inquiry.* Participants are expected to review areas of their own classroom practice. This unit provides advice on how to carry out such inquiries.

MODULE 2 – SPECIAL NEEDS: DEFINITIONS AND RESPONSES

STUDY MATERIAL 2:

This material provides an account of changes in thinking that are influencing developments in many countries. These changes redefine special needs in terms of the curriculum. They require teachers to develop their practice in order to help all pupils to learn. Pupils experiencing difficulty can be seen more positively as providing feedback on existing classroom arrangements. Improvements made in response to this feedback will be to the benefit of all pupils. Responding positively to special needs is a way of improving schools for all.

UNITS IN MODULE 2:

2.1 *Defining special needs.* Special needs are seen as arising from an interaction of a range of factors, some within the child, some in the community and, critically, others related to the responses of schools. This activity helps teachers to recognize these factors.

2.2 *What can schools do about special needs?* This exercise is intended to pinpoint those factors in schools that influence pupil learning and which, therefore, can be manipulated to overcome difficulties.

2.3 *Inclusive schools.* Throughout the world there are examples of schools that are successful in responding positively to pupil diversity. Studying these schools can help us to develop our understanding.

2.4 *Dealing with disabilities.* Inevitably special needs occur when schools are unable to deal with children's disabilities. Child studies are used as a basis for considering strategies for dealing with disability in schools.

2.5 *Attitudes to disability.* This unit provides an opportunity to consider different attitudes to disability. It also helps individuals to review their own thinking.

2.6 *Perspectives on disability.* An exercise in which teachers have the opportunity to meet disabled adults and discuss their experiences in school. Visual aids may also be used to help participants to become familiar with people who have disabilities.

2.7 *Integration in action.* Using a series of stories written by teachers in different parts of the world, this unit begins to identify the important features of practice that are important for dealing with special needs in ordinary schools.

2.8 *Looking at integration.* Based on school visits, this unit continues the investigation into good practice in dealing with special needs.

2.9 *The needs of teachers.* Assuming a curriculum view of special needs, there has to be consideration of the professional needs of teachers. Teachers who feel confident in themselves are better placed to respond to difficulties experienced by their pupils. This unit looks at ways in which teachers should deal with personal stress.

MODULE 3 – TOWARDS EFFECTIVE SCHOOLS FOR ALL

STUDY MATERIAL 3:

This material explores the practical implications of adopting a curriculum view of educational difficulties. The concern is on responding to individual pupils within a common curriculum rather than devising separate programmes. Given this argument, the question is: How can teachers improve their practice with respect to ways of responding to individuals within a class? The emphasis is on learning from experience, using colleagues to provide support and stimulation in establishing a reflective attitude. This being the case, there is also a need to establish strategies for evaluating classroom practice and responding on the basis of information collected. It is also very important to adopt a whole-school policy that gives support to individual teachers.

UNITS IN MODULE 3:

3.1 *Assessing and recording progress.* What is recorded in a classroom tends to have a major impact on the curriculum provided. This unit looks at orientations to assessment and recording, and includes a consideration of some examples.

3.2 *Making learning more meaningful.* Difficulties in learning occur when pupils perceive the curriculum as being irrelevant or lacking in meaning. Principles of good curriculum practice are presented and used as a means of evaluating the appropriateness of provision made in the classrooms of course participants.

3.3 *Changing practice.* The issue of change in education is considered. If teachers are to develop their own practice, they need to recognize the difficulties they face and the conditions that facilitate change.

3.4 *Classroom factors.* This unit examines some of the methods teachers use to respond to individual pupils in their classes. These factors provide an agenda within which course participants can consider their own current practice.

3.5 *Analysing classroom practice.* Using systematic observations of classroom practice this unit seeks to examine in more detail the factors that facilitate the progress of individual pupils.

3.6 *Co-operative learning.* There is increasing evidence to suggest that co-operative learning strategies are effective in helping pupils to achieve their academic goals. They can also facilitate the integration of exceptional pupils and encourage personal and social development.

3.7 *Structuring group activities.* Co-operative learning is only successful when group activities are planned to encourage positive interdependence between group members. This unit looks at practical strategies for using group learning in the classroom.

3.8 *Reading for learning.* Classroom reading material can cause particular difficulties for some children. This unit examines strategies for helping all pupils to read more effectively.

3.9 *Problem solving.* Whilst the main emphasis is on improving the curriculum, there is still the occasional need to devise additional responses to help pupils overcome particular difficulties. This unit provides a framework for the development of such responses.

3.10 *Putting it together.* This unit provides an opportunity for participants to use ideas from the other units to devise, implement and evaluate a lesson plan.

MODULE 4 – HELP AND SUPPORT

STUDY MATERIAL 4:
Whilst the importance of self-help is stressed throughout this project, the value of support should not be underestimated. Effective teachers recognize the importance of developing a support network. In particular they are skilful in gaining help from their pupils, their colleagues, parents and others in the community, and, where available, external support agencies. Successful schools have a commitment to collaboration as a means of creating positive learning conditions for pupils *and* teachers.

UNITS IN MODULE 4:

4.1 *Social climate of the classroom.* Successful teachers create an atmosphere in their classrooms that encourages learning. Such an atmosphere also reduces disruption. This unit explores these issues.

4.2 *Problem behaviour.* This unit considers ways of responding to behaviour that interferes with learning. It builds upon the problem-solving approach presented in Unit 3.9.

4.3 *Child-to-child.* This unit introduces participants to the thinking and practice of 'Child-to-child', an approach to peer tutoring that is used successfully in many parts of the world.

4.4 *Peer tutoring*. A range of strategies for encouraging children to help one another in the classroom are introduced in this unit, particularly paired reading.

4.5 *Partnership teaching*. There is considerable evidence to show the value of teachers collaborating in order to develop their practice. This has been shown to be a particularly powerful means of supporting individuals as they attempt to implement new ways of working in their classrooms.

4.6 *Sharing classrooms*. The presence of more than one adult in the classroom provides the basis for a more flexible range of responses to individual pupils. It can also present additional difficulties, however, particularly where the partnership is not well planned. This unit examines strategies for sharing classrooms successfully.

4.7 *Parents as partners*. Research has also shown the impact that parents can have upon the progress of their children. Seeing parents as partners in the process of learning is essential to this approach. Strategies for developing positive relationships between home and school are explored in this unit.

4.8 *Meeting parents*. Meetings between parents and teachers can be stressful for both groups. In this unit ways of making such meetings more positive will be examined.

4.9 *Community involvement*. This unit looks at the relationships between schools and the communities they serve. It is argued that successful education requires a shared understanding as to the purposes of the curriculum. On a more pragmatic level, the resources of the wider community should be available as a source of support to teachers.

4.10 *External agencies*. Whilst the availability of external support agencies varies from area to area, it is important to recognize that the key issue is to make effective use of those that are available. This unit looks at strategies for setting up appropriate forms of communication with other professionals.

4.11 *Practice and feedback*. The materials in the resource pack can be used in a variety of settings, including as part of school development. This unit provides an opportunity for participants to practise using sections of the pack for teacher development activities.

PLANNING SESSIONS

Whilst the instruction sheets associated with each of the units give suggestions for activities, it is necessary to plan in more detail what types of teaching and learning approaches to use. In constructing an overall plan for a course or workshop, care should be taken to use a range of approaches in order to take account of different preferences amongst participants and as a means of offering a degree of variety.

Chapter 5

Encouraging Teacher Development

In the earlier chapters we have reconstructed special needs as a task of school improvement. Central to this task is the work of teachers. Consequently, our concern is with finding ways of helping teachers to respond positively to educational difficulties in order to develop their classroom practice.

Through the work of the UNESCO project we have come to recognize the importance of *two* major strategies that seem to be effective in helping teachers to adopt the wider, curriculum perspective on educational difficulties: *reflective inquiry* and *collaboration*. Furthermore, we have formulated and refined five sets of approaches that seem to be successful in creating teacher education contexts that encourage teachers and student teachers to adopt the two strategies.

In this chapter we provide a detailed explanation of the kinds of teacher education approaches that we find useful. Whilst these approaches are essential for those making use of the Resource Pack, they also provide a bank of ideas that will be relevant to anybody wishing to develop effective teacher education initiatives. Experience shows that these approaches can be adapted to fit in with different contexts, including pre-service and in-service education initiatives.

Before looking in detail at the five sets of recommended approaches some rather general remarks about the use of the Resource Pack are required.

USING THE RESOURCE PACK

The emphasis placed on flexibility when using the Resource Pack means that it can be used in a number of teacher-education settings. For example:

1. *Pre-service courses.* The materials can be used as an element of pre-service courses for student teachers. This might take the form of a distinct component dealing with special educational needs. Alternatively, the materials and activities could be integrated into other courses about classroom practice. In many ways this latter option is more consistent with the general philosophy of the pack. Where the materials are used with student teachers, it is particularly important that they have opportunities to visit schools in order to observe classroom practice and carry out practical assignments based upon course activities. (Examples of this are provided in Chapter 6.)

2. *In-service courses.* These can take many forms and the flexibility of the materials will be helpful in this respect. The materials could, for example, be used as the basis of a one-week intensive course for teachers drawn from a series of schools. Alternatively, a series of weekly sessions might be offered over a period of months. This approach would be particularly helpful in that participants could undertake practical activities related to the course in their own classrooms. Participants might also be encouraged to use the course materials to run similar sessions back in their own schools for their colleagues. (Accounts of in-service use of the pack are provided in Chapter 7.)

3. *School-based staff development.* This approach may be a particularly valuable way of using the Resource Pack. The idea would be to use the materials and activities to stage a series of sessions for all teachers in a school. They would be encouraged to use these sessions to review school policy and practice, and to plan developments. The strength of this approach is that it addresses real issues faced in a particular context and that it encourages long-term collaboration between members of a school's staff. (Chapter 8 provides examples of school-based projects.)

Before considering the specific instructions on setting up the activities associated with each module it is worth thinking about some general issues. Throughout the course the aim is to encourage participants to reflect upon their own thinking and consider their existing practice as teachers. Consequently you should seek to create a comfortable and relaxed working atmosphere. To help with this you should:

1. Read the notes provided for each activity and ensure that you have all necessary materials to hand.

2. Check the timetable for the session. There is a lot to get through and it is important to leave sufficient time for individuals to reflect upon what they have been doing.

3. Arrange seating for your group ina way that will encourage a relaxed atmosphere. A circle of chairs is probably the best arrangement.

4. Start the first session by asking each member of the group to introduce himself/herself. Establish the use of first names, including you own, and try to use names frequently in order that participants have plenty of chance to learn what other people are called.

5. Draw attention to the aims of the session and how it is to develop.

6. Encourage a willingness to listen to other people's opinions and ideas.

7. Experienced teachers may feel nervous and uncertain when asked to consider new ideas. Try to overcome this by providing reassurance and encouragement as contributions are made.

8. Do not get into heated arguments with individuals in the group. If you feel that somebody is taking too narrow a view, ask him or her to consider an alternative, or get somebody else in the group to put forward a different position. At all costs, avoid blunt criticism, ridicule and sarcasm.

9. Other participants may continually stress practical difficulties (for instance class size; naughty children and pressure of work) which seem to make the course proposals unrealistic. Accept that these do exist but encourage the group to come up with ways of getting around them.

Finally, it cannot be stressed too much that as a workshop leader your main role is to make the whole experience of attending the course a pleasant useful one. In the words of the poet John Masefield,

'The days that make us happy make us wise'.

Figure 5.1 Notes for Course Leaders Using the Resource Pack 'Special Needs in the Classroom'

Whatever the content and format, it is important that course leaders and participants agree about arrangements for the course. This may mean the course leader providing a detailed programme for participants based upon the materials in the pack. Alternatively, the course leader and participants may negotiate a suitable programme as a result of an examination of what the pack offers. The outline provided on pages 10–13 of the Resource Pack can be used to inform such negotiations.

Throughout the preliminary stages of setting up a course, it is important to stress the style that will be adopted throughout. Attention should be drawn to the overall aim, particularly the phrase 'to help teachers to develop their thinking and practice'. Similarly the ideas of participants taking responsibility for their own learning should be discussed. This approach may be very new to participants and they will need help in understanding the implications.

---

1. Active learning

    1.1 Forming working groups

    1.2 Brainstorming

    1.3 Nominal group techniques

    1.4 Structured problem-solving

    1.5 Stance taking

    1.6 Using written texts

    1.7 Variety of methods

    1.8 Inquiry

    1.9 The jigsaw classroom

2. Negotiation of objectives

    2.1 Making aims clear

    2.2 Choosing the focus

    2.3 Learning journals

    2.4 Negotiated programme

    2.5 Twos and fours

    2.6 Stone walls

    2.7 Decision-making

Figure 5.2 Approaches Used with the UNESCO Resource Pack 'Special Needs in the Classroom'

3. Demonstration, practice and feedback

    3.1   Modelling

    3.2   Classroom implementation

    3.3   Partnership teaching

    3.4   Contracts

    3.5   Visits

    3.6   Videos or slides

    3.7   Teams

4. Continuous evaluation

    4.1   Thinking time

    4.2   Active listening

    4.3   Rounds

    4.4   Group feedback

    4.5   Spokesperson

    4.6   Statements

    4.7   Debriefing

    4.8   Evaluation

    4.9   Conferencing

5. Support

    5.1   Visiting classes

    5.2   Breaking the ice

    5.3   Ground rules

    5.4   Interdependence

    5.5   Positive feedback

    5.6   Informal mixing

    5.7   Seating arrangements

    5.8   Using names

Figure 5.2 Approaches Used with the UNESCO Resource Pack 'Special Needs in the Classroom' (continued)

The role of course leader is crucial to the success of any initiative of this sort. In this case it is particularly important that the course leader acts in a manner that is consistent with the aims and strategies that are central to the Resource Pack. The notes overleaf (Figure 5.1) are intended to help course leaders plan their work.

The approaches associated with the UNESCO Resource Pack are not comprehensive. Those who use the pack are encouraged to devise their own ways of working. Figure 5.2 summarizes the approaches we recommend.

1. ACTIVE LEARNING

Here we are looking for approaches that encourage participants in a course session to engage with opportunities for learning. A particular emphasis is placed on various forms of group work as a means of helping participants to learn from one another. The approaches we recommend are as follows:

1.1. FORMING WORKING GROUPS

The use of various kinds of working groups is an essential approach for teacher development activities. Group work provides opportunities for individuals to think about their own practice, hear alternative points of view and work collaboratively to create new solutions to practical problems. The intention is that participants should, through the experience of a course or workshop, see the value of working with their colleagues. Furthermore, participants are encouraged to transfer these collaborative practices into their usual workplace.

However, for this to be successful it is vital that care be taken when forming working groups. Participants who are not used to this type of approach may be embarrassed or even threatened by being asked to form themselves into teams. Consequently, the course leader must be sensitive and, at the same time, firm in making appropriate arrangements.

There are many different ways in which groups can be formed. For example, participants may be asked to number around the room (e.g. 1 to 6, where six groups are required) and then told to meet up with those participants who have the same number. Alternatively, they may all be asked to stand in a long line across the room, with the order determined by the initials of their first names or their height. They then number off into groups of appropriate size for the task to be carried out.

Group size is an important factor. Initially, whilst participants are getting to know one another, smaller groups are preferable (i.e. two or three members in each group). Later it may be possible to use larger size groups. However, groups of six tend to be the maximum if all individuals are going to contribute to the discussions and activities.

Finally it is advisable to keep reforming the groups so that participants have opportunities to meet all course members.

1.2. BRAINSTORMING

This approach is valuable in creating an agenda for discussion within a working group. It involves a set period when participants suggest points or comments relating to the area under discussion. One member of the group records these contributions, preferably on a blackboard or overhead projector. Strict rules are kept during the brainstorming in order that participants feel confident to make their suggestions without fear of criticism. Essential rules are:

- all ideas related to the issue in any direct way are desired
- a maximum number of related ideas is desired
- one idea may be modified, adapted and expressed as another idea
- ideas should be expressed as clearly and concisely as possible
- no discussion of the ideas should be attempted and
- no criticism of ideas is accepted.

Once the brainstorming period is over, the list of points generated provides an agenda for normal discussion.

1.3 NOMINAL GROUP TECHNIQUES

This is a more sophisticated strategy for structuring group discussion. Its strengths are that it:

- ensures that all participants contribute
- avoids the dominance of a few people who have particularly strong views
- encourages a flexible interpretation of the issue under consideration
- ensures a wide range of responses and
- allows a systematic ordering of priorities.

The technique requires a group leader who must remain neutral throughout the activity. The procedure is carried out as follows:

1. Clarification of the task. The task is presented on a blackboard or overhead projector (e.g. 'What aspects of the curriculum do we need to reconsider?'). In order that all participants fully understand the question, time is spent in group discussion about the nature of the task.
2. Silent nominations. Individuals are given a fixed period to list their own private responses. This should not be hurried. They are then asked to rank their own list in order to establish felt priorities.
3. Master list. The group leader compiles a master list on the blackboard or overhead projector taking one item from each group member in rotation. No editing of the material is allowed and no evaluative comments are to be made at this stage. It is helpful to number the items.
4. Item classification. During this phase each item is discussed until all members know what it means. Clarification only is allowed. If a member of the group now feels that their item is already covered by someone else's, they may request its withdrawal. No pressure should be applied to any individual to have items withdrawn or incorporated in another.
5. Evaluation. It is now necessary to decide the relative importance of items in the eyes of the group. Each person is allowed five weighted votes (five points for the item that is felt to be most important, four points for the next, and so on). A simple voting procedure allows the consensus to emerge.

Once the composite picture has emerged, it provides an agenda for normal group discussions to proceed.

1.4 STRUCTURED PROBLEM-SOLVING

This approach is particularly advantageous when reviewing what has been achieved with a view to deciding what are the problems and how best these can be overcome. The steps involved are as follows:

1. Groups of three are set up. One of the participants takes on the role of 'explainer' and the other two act as 'clarifiers'. The

'explainer' explains what they have done and the problems they have encountered. It is then the job of the 'clarifiers' to ensure that what is being said is fully understood by all. They should not pass value judgements.

2. The role of 'explainer' rotates so that all three get a chance to discuss what they have been doing.
3. After each person has discussed what they have been doing, an agreed list of difficulties facing each one is drawn up. Each difficulty is then itemized on a separate card.
4. The sets of cards are passed to another member of the group, who in turn reviews the difficulty stated on the card and then on the reverse tries to complete the sentence 'Have you considered…'.
5. This process is repeated with another member of the group.
6. The responses are reviewed by the whole group.

1.5. STANCE-TAKING

In this approach two groups prepare opposite sides of an argument about a matter of concern (the integration of children with disabilities for instance). Pairs are then formed of individuals from each group and they present their arguments to one another. Through this process individuals are helped to have a further understanding of the complexities of the issue.

1.6 USING WRITTEN TEXTS

Some participants may find certain course materials difficult to understand. In this case active group approaches will be valuable. There are a number of such approaches, all rooted in the view that reading should be seen as a strategy for learning. This involves decoding a text, making sense of what it is saying and relating this to the reader's existing understanding. By these processes judgements are made, and knowledge is extended and modified. In other words, this is how learning takes place.

The main strategy is to encourage participants to work collaboratively in pairs or small groups to gain meaning from written materials. To help with this they are introduced to procedures for analysing a written text. So, for example, they may be asked to work with a partner to:

1. Locate and identify particular information in the material (This may involve underlining parts of the text to indicate where particular information can be found.).
2. Mark the located information in some way as an aid to understanding (here sections of the text may be grouped into categories of particular significance).
3. Organize the information and present it in a different form, perhaps by making a list of items located in the text or by filling in information on some form of table or graph.

Groups may also be asked to consider questions or issues that are not dealt with in the text, or not dealt with adequately. This may well require them to think beyond the actual written material by considering questions such as 'What might have happened if...?' or 'What would be the result of...?'

Other useful techniques involve some modifications of the texts to be used. For example:

1. activities that involve the group in completing material that has words or sections deleted
2. the presentation of a text cut up into separate sentences or paragraphs that the group have to put into sequence
3. prediction of likely outcomes before going on to read the next page or section.

A further technique that can be useful in helping readers to find meaning in difficult material is known as SQ3R. This involves teaching study skills involving the following processes.

Survey. An initial rapid sampling of the material to stimulate interest and give a sense of direction to subsequent intensive reading.

Question. At the same time as this initial contact, questions are formulated which are intended to promote anticipation of, and prediction from, the material to be read.

Read. Having surveyed the material and discussed questions raised, detailed reading should be an active search rather than a passive read.

Review. This involves organizing and reviewing what has been learned from the text and taking steps to prevent forgetting.

Recite. Finally the content is recited in order to demonstrate understanding. Once again this approach is best carried out as a collaborative exercise.

1.7. VARIETY OF METHODS

Whilst group activities are very effective in creating positive learning conditions, it is important to provide a variety of learning contexts, thereby accommodating the preferences of individual participants. The aim is to cater for diversity by offering a range of contexts and, as a result, help participants to become more aware of their own learning preferences.

Thus, in addition to group work of various kinds, use should be made of individual activities such as silent reading, writing or drawing; visits; audio-visual stimulus materials; or lecture presentations. Particular course members who are known to have significant experience or expertise may be requested to give short talks to the whole group.

In planning a course or workshop, therefore, attention should be given to providing a variety of learning opportunities. This is a powerful means of encouraging active engagement in the topic under consideration. In particular, it makes sense to utilize considerable variety at times when participants can be expected to be tired, towards the end of the day, or during after-school staff development activities for instance.

1.8. INQUIRY

As we have stressed already, inquiry is a central mode of learning for teachers. We are keen to encourage the idea that all teachers should see it as their responsibility to improve their practice. Essential to this is that they find ways of reflecting upon their existing ways of working. In this respect we want them to use the feedback of those pupils who experience difficulties in learning, as a means of gaining insight as to how their own practice might be improved.

Inquiry need not involve the use of technical instruments, although these may be useful on some occasions. Rather, it requires an attitude of mind whereby teachers attempt to make sense of what they see and hear as they work with their classes. Writing about their observations and discussing them with colleagues are useful ways of analysing what is significant.

Where more specific inquiry methods are necessary and feasible, five techniques are likely to be relevant:

- Classroom observation
- Interviews
- Meetings
- Questionnaires
- Analysis of documents.

Guidelines on using these methods are provided in Unit 1.6 of the UNESCO Resource Pack.

1.9 THE JIGSAW CLASSROOM

One way to structure positive interdependence among group members is to use the jigsaw method of creating resource interdependence. There are five basic steps for structuring a 'jigsaw' activity.

1. Distribute a set of materials to each group. The set needs to be divisible into the number of members of the group (two, three, or four parts). Give each member one part of the set of materials.
2. Assign participants individual tasks:
    - Learning and becoming an expert on their material.
    - Planing how to teach the material to the other members of the group.
3. Assign participants the task of meeting with someone else in the class who is a member of another learning group and who has learned the same material. They are to share ideas as to how the material may best be taught. This is known as an 'expert pair' or 'expert group'.
4. Assign students the co-operative tasks of:
    - Teaching their area of expertise to the other group members.
    - Learning the material being taught by the other members.
5. Help participants to debrief the activity.

Various adaptations can be made of the jigsaw approach.

2. NEGOTIATION OF OBJECTIVES

These are approaches that enable teacher development activities to take account of the concerns and interests of individual participants. They include the following:

2.1. MAKING AIMS CLEAR

This suggestion is obvious and straightforward, yet too often it is not used. Before each activity it is important to explain the aim to all participants. This may also involve a discussion of why the aim is significant. At this stage, participants may comment or even disagree with the course leader. It may be necessary, therefore, to discuss whether the activity is relevant to the course participants. If it is not, it seems pointless to proceed.

2.2. CHOOSING THE FOCUS

The topics for particular sessions are usually planned by the course leaders, taking account of negotiations with group members. In addition, ways should be found that enable participants to address their own agendas. In other words, we want participants to draw upon their own experience, consider their own concerns and determine the specific issues that they wish to address.

This can be achieved by asking participants to read study material prior to a course session. For example, they may be given a short handout of background material and asked to study it before they come to the course. They may also be asked to prepare some short written comments relating the content of the handout to their own experience and concerns. It is important to stress that participants must carry out these assignments. Otherwise the session will get off to a bad start whilst they attempt to catch up with their homework.

Sometimes the focus of discussion is decided within each working group. For example, groups may be asked to choose the particular aspect of a topic that they would like to discuss. In this way activities are made more directly relevant to course members.

2.3. LEARNING JOURNALS

This takes the form of a diary, a personal document in which participants write about their own learning. One element may be for participants to write about their own priorities within the course – areas of their own thinking and practice that they are seeking to develop. Essentially the idea is to encourage participants to take responsibility for their own learning. It may be helpful to allow short periods during the course for writing in the journal. Participants may also be asked to read extracts aloud (this should be optional, however). Another possibility would be to give suggested headings to encourage the writing process, such as the following

- Ideas to be remembered
- Questions requiring thought
- Leads to follow up
- Points to share with colleagues
- Reactions to the session.

2.4. NEGOTIATED PROGRAMME

One way in which individual objectives can be negotiated and accommodated for within a course would be for the course leader to negotiate the whole programme with the participants. In this way the course can be designed to take account of the professional concerns and interests of the course members. Using an outline programme, participants discuss possible options and then agree the content and issues to be addressed. The course leader, of course, contributes his or her point of view in this decision-making procedure.

2.5. TWOS AND FOURS

This is a very useful approach for encouraging individuals to discuss their own learning objectives. It is also generally a good way of encouraging discussion. First, the group discuss the issues in pairs. Then two pairs join up to compare notes and to try to come to some joint agreement about their position. Finally, the various groups join together for discussion. The advantage of this approach is that the views of all individuals are expressed at some stage.

2.6. STONE WALLS

This is an approach that can be particularly valuable towards the end of a course. The aim is to help participants define their future priorities and deal with possible obstacles. Individuals are asked to draw a simple mountain. At the top of the mountain they write down their objective (for instance 'To improve my use of co-operative learning in my classroom'). They then sketch a stone wall in front of their mountain. Each stone in the wall represents a possible obstacle that may prevent the individual climbing their mountain. Obstacles are written on to the stones. In small groups there is discussion in order to consider how the stones in the wall might be moved out of the way. Participants may also be asked to consider how far the obstacles are of their own making.

2.7. DECISION-MAKING

Many course activities involve decision-making. Groups may be asked to choose a focus for their decisions, a way of operating or, very often, to come to some conclusions as a result of their deliberations. Some activities in particular are planned in order to provide opportunities for practising group problem-solving techniques. Consequently, it is necessary to help participants to improve their skills in this area.

There are five major characteristics of an effective decision.

1. The resources of group members are fully utilized.
2. Time is well used.
3. The decision is correct or of high quality (a high-quality decision solves the problem, can be implemented in a way that the problem does not reoccur and does not require more time, people and material resources than the school can provide).
4. All the required staff members are fully committed to implementing the decision.
5. The problem-solving ability of the group is enhanced, or at least not reduced.

Decisions can be made in a number of ways. Whenever possible, however, key policy and planning decisions should be made by consensus. This is the most effective procedure, but it also takes the most time.

3. DEMONSTRATION, PRACTICE AND FEEDBACK

The following approaches are intended to model examples of practice, encourage their use in the classroom and provide supportive feedback:

3.1. MODELLING

The role of the course leader involves using these techniques as a means of facilitating the learning of course participants. Many of the activities will require the course leader to demonstrate effective ways of running the group in a way that encourages the involvement of individuals. Then, as the course proceeds, individual participants will have opportunities within the group to take the lead during the sessions. Whenever appropriate, discussion of these sessions should be used as a means of giving participants *positive* feedback about their contributions. Course leaders should also seek feedback on the way they are running the course sessions.

3.2. CLASSROOM IMPLEMENTATION

The most difficult task for participants is to take ideas heard during course sessions and incorporate them into their existing repertoire of approaches. Too often this crucial aspect is left to chance. A much better way is to get participants to help one another to plan how they might try out new approaches. So, for example, following a session on the use of praise in the classroom, participants might discuss how they might review their own practice with respect to this matter.

Attention should be given during sessions to the debriefing of these implementation activities. Indeed, it is through the debriefing of such activities that course sessions can be enriched. As individuals talk about what they have tried, other course members have the opportunity to hear the outcomes and compare these with their own experiences.

3.3. PARTNERSHIP TEACHING

As participants try out new approaches in their classroom or, indeed, attempt to inquire into aspects of their existing practice, it is important to set up supportive arrangements. Too often individual teachers are left to carry out these classroom implementation activities alone. Establishing partnerships can provide this in-class support as a powerful staff development strategy. Three forms of partnership are worthy of consideration.

1. *Peer observation.* Peer observation refers to the observation of one's teaching by another (usually a friendly colleague). It is now fairly well established that teachers learn best from other teachers and take criticism most easily from this source. It is ideal if teachers in peer groups can act as observers for each other; this mutual exchange of roles quickly breaks down barriers and encourages collaboration.

   Observers can play any number of differing roles. They can focus on specific aspects of the teaching and talk to pupils all during one observation period. In addition they may note incidents that the teacher would ordinarily miss.

2. *Clinical supervision.* Clinical supervision is a technique that has enjoyed much popularity in North America, where it was developed as a method of supervising student teachers, but it is also suited for use in classroom research situations. It is a more structured form of peer observation that focuses on a teacher's performance, utilizing a three-phase approach to the observation of teaching events.

   The three essential phases of the clinical supervision process are a planning conference, classroom observation and a feedback conference. The planning conference provides the observer and teacher with an opportunity to reflect on the proposed lesson, and this leads to a mutual decision to collect observational data on an aspect of the teacher's teaching. During the classroom observation phase, the observer observes the teacher teach and collects objective data on that aspect of teaching agreed upon earlier. In the feedback conference, the observer and teacher share information, decide on possible actions (if necessary) and often plan to collect further observational data. It is important to realize that, to be effective, all three phases of the process need to be gone through systematically.

3. *Peer coaching.* Peer coaching is a teacher-to-teacher interaction aimed at improving teaching. Because of its personal nature, a

climate of trust needs to be established. Partners select each other and work on problems voluntarily; they must not feel that their confidentiality will be breached. The primary purpose of peer coaching is support, not evaluation; thus, peers are more appropriate partners than administrators in this professional growth scheme.

3.4. CONTRACTS

Where pairs of teachers (within the course or back in school) are working collaboratively in order to help one another to develop an aspect of their teaching, it makes sense to have an agreement as to how this will be carried out. Such an agreement should establish trust between partners, dealing with matters related to decision-making and confidentiality. It should also ensure that feedback between colleagues emphasizes positive achievements.

3.5. VISITS

The opportunity to visit other teachers' classrooms can be a powerful training experience. Seeing others at work, watching how they deal with problems in their classrooms, can help participants to review their own practice. Seeing 'good' practice can also be a source of inspiration and confidence. It is helpful to know that what you are trying to do in your own classroom already happens elsewhere. A number of the units require visits to observe practice. It is important that these are well prepared and then, afterwards, debriefed.

3.6. VIDEOS OR SLIDES

Visits are not always possible and consequently, other ways of observing examples of classroom practice have to be found. Slides or, even better, video extracts are valuable alternatives. With this in mind, the UNESCO Resource Pack includes video programmes showing examples of schools in different parts of the world that are able to cater for pupil diversity successfully.

Prior to viewing slides or video material, participants should be given a clear purpose. For example, they might be told, 'As you watch this extract of a school try to note ways in which the teachers respond to pupils who experience learning difficulties'.

Having viewed the material, participants may be asked to talk in pairs in order to share reactions and compare notes. Following on from these initial discussions the course leader can then take feedback and encourage further whole-group discussions.

3.7. TEAMS

Where appropriate, course participants should be encouraged to create development teams with a colleague or colleagues in their own schools. These teams can then provide help and support to individual members as they attempt to implement new approaches in their own classrooms.

To be effective a team requires:

1. Valid and complete information about the approaches being tried.
2. Enough intellectual conflict and disagreement to ensure that alternative potential points of view get a fair hearing.
3. A method of analysis and synthesis that generates ideas for improvement.
4. Free and informed choice.
5. Continuing motivation to solve problems if the implemented plan does not work.

4. CONTINUOUS EVALUATION

These approaches encourage enquiry and reflection as ways of reviewing the learning of course participants.

4.1. THINKING TIME

A simple strategy that can be very helpful in encouraging participants to reflect upon their own learning is simply to be silent. Allowing silence within a session requires the confidence of the course leader, since it can create a sense of unease amongst the group. Nevertheless, thinking time can be very beneficial in the midst of or at the end of a busy activity. The evaluation issues noted in each unit may prove a useful focus for reflections of this type.

4.2. ACTIVE LISTENING

In this approach course participants are asked to work in pairs. Each partner is then given a fixed time to reflect upon a session or activity (usually two minutes). They are invited to think about what has happened, what they have enjoyed and what they might like to do later as a result of this experience. Whilst one partner talks, the other is required to listen actively. For this purpose active listening involves:

- looking at the person who is talking
- sitting quietly
- doing nothing else but listening
- responding naturally with gestures and expressions
- making no comments
- only asking a question if clarification of a point.

4.3. ROUNDS

A round is a time when each person in the circle has an opportunity to make a statement about whatever the group is discussing. One person starts and the turns move round the circle; no one may comment on what anyone else says – and this includes the leader. Anyone can say 'I pass' when it is their turn.

The aim of the round is to provide a structure within which everyone has a chance to say something, but is not forced to do so. All ideas and opinions are valued equally. When rounds are first introduced, many people may say 'I pass'. Initially, no comment should be made about this as the choice must be free; but, if it continues to be a problem, the group may need to discuss it together. Usually the number of passes decreases as the participants realize that they can speak freely without fear of ridicule.

The round may often be a good way to start a session; it provides 're-entry' – members of the group get to know each other again and the feeling of safety is re-established in the circle. A good round to do in this situation would be 'The best thing that happened to me this week was…'. The round can be used at any point where an expression of opinion, or feedback, or planning, or evaluation is needed. So, at the end of a session, the group might do two rounds: 'What I didn't like about this session…' (Resent) and 'What I liked about this session…' (Appreciate). It is a good idea to do the negative round first, leaving the group with a positive feeling.

Remember, the freedom not to participate is extremely important in establishing trust. It is also important that no-one is interrupted and that no-one, including the leader, comments, positively or negatively, on anyone else's contribution while a round is in progress.

4.4. GROUP FEEDBACK

It is occasionally useful to ask small groups to discuss the course. They might be asked to make a list of 'highs' and 'lows'. In other words, they list things that they find useful and enjoyable, on the one hand, and things about which they are less happy, on the other. A spokesperson from each group then reads out the 'highs' and the 'lows'. This can be useful in helping the course leader to plan further sessions.

4.5. SPOKESPERSON

When working groups have come to some conclusion about their assigned tasks, they may be asked to make a report to the rest of the course members. Individuals may be asked to give these reports, possibly by using a poster or flip chart to illustrate the key ideas. Such a spokesperson may be a volunteer, somebody nominated by the course leader, or an individual selected by the group.

Making such a presentation provides an opportunity for the individual to think aloud, revisiting and reviewing what was discussed in the working group and, as a result clarify their own thinking.

4.6. STATEMENTS

Statements are written reports prepared by individual participants, related to their own learning. They should be positive in nature, emphasizing what has been achieved so far. They might also include a list of priorities for further development. It helps if individual participants can have a few moments to discuss their statements in private with the course leader.

4.7. DEBRIEFING

Debriefing of group activities is a vital aspect of a course leader's work. It is the means by which all participants can be helped to make sense of a complex learning activity and record their own learning. It is also very demanding on course leaders, requiring them to summarize the outcome of the various activities, discussions and group reports that have occurred. Usually this takes place towards the end of a session when course leaders (as well as participants) may well be feeling tired.

During the field-testing of the UNESCO Resource Pack, the co-ordinators frequently referred to being exhausted at the end of a course day. Clearly the approaches we are recommending are very demanding, and for course leaders, the summarizing of sessions may well be the most demanding task of all. It requires them to listen carefully, analyse what they hear and then almost instantly provide a coherent summary of the main ideas. Furthermore, this is a process that cannot be prepared before the session since it has to be based upon the events that occur.

This being said, our experience is that as course leaders become familiar with this way of working the tendency to exhaustion is reduced. Apart from anything else, involvement with previous course groups that have discussed similar topics means that course leaders are able to anticipate at least some of the likely outcomes.

4.8. EVALUATION FORMS

In addition to these various interactive evaluation processes, it may be useful sometimes to ask participants to complete a questionnaire or schedule. Figure 5.3 is an example of the schedules we use within the UNESCO project. These may be used during a course for planning purposes, or afterwards in order to carry out an analysis of the effects of the course. Sometimes information collected in this way is analysed by working groups which then summarize their findings for the whole course group.

4.9. CONFERENCING

This is a term used to describe an extended discussion between a participant and the course leader. Conferencing is similar to conducting an informal interview. Such a session offers an opportunity for teacher and student to come to a mutual understanding of the nature of work in progress and to discuss what has been found to be enjoyable/not enjoyable or easy/challenging/hard. It also provides a chance to discuss any difficulties which are being experienced and to plan future activities. Such discussions should also allow them to talk about the activities and their feelings towards them. Conferencing can contribute greatly to an openly-negotiated working consensus.

Participants' Questionnaire

We would like your views about various aspects of the course. It will help us in improving future sessions. Please complete the following sentences:

1. The most useful part of the course was…
2. I liked…
3. I did not like…
4. I felt the methods were…
5. The content of the course was…
6. The materials we used were…
7. As a result of this course, I…
8. I also feel that…

THANK YOU FOR YOUR HELP

Figure 5.3 – Example of an evaluation form

5. SUPPORT

As we have seen, the approaches recommended are very demanding for participants and course leaders.

Consequently, it is vital to balance the deliberate pressure with systematic arrangements for support. The following approaches are helpful in this respect:

5.1. VISITING CLASSES

An important aspect of the course leader's work is to find ways of helping participants to create links with normal classroom practice. A helpful approach here is for course leaders to visit participants in their usual workplace. These visits may be conducted prior to, during or after the course. They may simply be short diplomatic visits or, if time allows, involve planned activities to support participants with their work.

Apart from the value of such visits as a means of helping course leaders to take account of the concerns of participants, they also help to encourage supportive relationships.

5.2. BREAKING THE ICE

The early meetings of a new course group are vital in creating a positive working atmosphere. Inevitably at this stage participants will be uncertain about what is to happen and possibly uncertain about their own capacity to cope. Furthermore, these feelings may be made worse by the nature of the approaches made and may be very different to those experienced previously.

Consequently, it is helpful during early sessions to encourage participants to get to know one another quickly. Small group discussions are obviously helpful in this respect. Participants should also be asked to say a few words before the whole group. For example, each person may be asked to say who they are, where they are from and how they would like to be addressed. They may also be asked to say in a lighthearted way something about themselves that will help the group to remember who they are.

It is vital that all these early activities are undertaken in a confident, informal and supportive style that will put participants at ease.

5.3. GROUND RULES

After a group has been working together for a while it may be useful to agree some ground rules. Sometimes an appropriate moment for this occurs as a result of something that is said during a session. In this way the group actually experiences the ground rules whilst engaged in introductory activities before they are asked to define them. What is wanted is a set of rules which will help to create and sustain the friendly and cohesive atmosphere that facilitates learning. Inevitably the group discussion towards formulating the rules will in itself encourage a supportive atmosphere. Examples of the sorts of rules that might be helpful include the following:

- We listen to each other
- We respect each other's ideas and values
- Participation is optional
- It is okay to make mistakes – they are valuable learning points
- We avoid hurting each other.

It is important that groups seek to establish rules that are meaningful and relevant.

5.4. INTERDEPENDENCE

One of the ways in which a supportive atmosphere can be created within a course is by asking participants to carry out tasks that require collaboration. This idea of creating interdependence is built into many of the activities in the pack. It can be helped along if course leaders pay attention to:

- the setting of tasks that necessitate collaboration
- helping participants to recognize that their learning can be helped by other members of the group
- group size and membership that is appropriate given the skills and experience of the participants and the nature of the tasks that are set
- the development of participants' skills in aspects of group working, including communication, sharing ideas and decision-making.

Groupwork that encourages interdependence can take a variety of forms. For example:

- pairs may read the study material together, discussing the content and preparing answers to given questions
- pairs may prepare a joint statement about a topic which they are responsible for presenting to a larger group

- a group may be involved in a task that can only be completed if the separate materials held by individuals are pooled
- group members may brainstorm ideas, which are recorded by one member who acts as scribe
- individual members of a group may be assigned particular roles, e.g. chairperson, recorder, summarizer, reporter.

In debriefing activities of this sort it is important to ask individuals what they have learned from the experience about working effectively in groups.

5.5. POSITIVE FEEDBACK

This point has already been made a number of times with reference to some of the earlier suggestions. Nevertheless it is important enough to be restated separately. We all appreciate it when somebody values our efforts by indicating their recognition and appreciation. One way in which a supportive atmosphere can be created within a group is by the leader responding positively to the contributions made by participants. A possible benefit of this is that participants may well be encouraged to make similar responses to their course leader!

5.6. INFORMAL MIXING

An important way of providing support is through the creation of a friendly, relaxed atmosphere. The nature and style of this will vary as a result of cultural traditions. Informality between students and teachers is not common in some countries.

Without wishing to change these conventions, it is still possible for course leaders to show their interest in their participants as individuals. Friendly conversations prior to, during and after a course session will usually be welcomed by participants. Taking an interest in how individuals are responding to the sessions is also a useful way of gaining feedback about the course. In addition, such discussions are a way of finding out things about participants that can be drawn on during course activities.

5.7. SEATING ARRANGEMENTS

The way a classroom is arranged gives important messages as to what is intended. Tables and chairs organized in rows that face the blackboard suggest that the mode of learning assumes that the interactions are likely to be mainly between the teacher and children.

Given that we wish to provide a variety of learning contexts in order to cater for the diversity of course participants, it is obvious that different room arrangements will be necessary. Often at the beginning of a session the groups will sit in a circle or half-circle to hear the aims and instructions for the activities that are to take place. Presentations involving a blackboard, overhead projector or video also dictate particular seating arrangements.

At other times, however, furniture will need to be moved around by participants to form the various working groups that are necessary. Sometimes tables may be needed to prepare group drawings or posters. Groups may also find it comfortable to work on the floor when carrying out such activities.

Clearly this type of flexibility is made easier in rooms that are relatively spacious and have light furniture.

5.8. USING NAMES

Unless it is unacceptable for cultural reasons, it is better to use first names within group sessions, thereby giving the message that this is a group of colleagues who have come together to help one another to learn successfully. Thus habitual formal relationships or differences of status are suspended for the specific purposes of the course. In such a context, all are equal since all are learners.

In addition, it is important to encourage the use of names. Thus the course leader should seek to learn the names of participants quickly and use them during sessions. This is a way of showing that all individuals are recognized and regarded as important members of the group. Similarly group members should be encouraged to learn one another's names. This again encourages participation and creates a supportive atmosphere. A helpful strategy here is to ask participants to spend a few minutes trying to name everybody in the group.

Chapter 6

Teacher Development at the Pre-Service Stage

The next three chapters provide accounts of the field-testing of the pilot version of the UNESCO Resource Pack 'Special Needs in the Classroom'. These accounts are adapted from the longer and much more detailed evaluation reports prepared by the members of the international resource team in the eight participating countries. Together they give an indication of the potential uses of the pack, illustrating in particular the importance of flexibility in order to respond to local circumstances. They also provide a wealth of practical ideas on the design of effective teacher education programmes.

The accounts are grouped together on the basis of the contexts in which the studies were undertaken. In this chapter, we look at pre-service teacher education; Chapter 7 is concerned with in-service education; Chapter 8 has examples of school-based staff development initiatives.

This chapter looks at three examples of attempts to use the Resource Pack at the pre-service stage. The first two, set in India and Kenya, show the potential of the pack for reforming teacher education in ways that link theory to practice. In both accounts successful attempts were made to encourage student teachers to try out the approaches being used in local schools. At times this led to difficulties, particularly where more experienced colleagues found the new approaches difficult to understand. These experiences point to the need for careful preparation of personnel when teacher education reforms are being introduced.

In this respect the third account from Zimbabwe is particularly interesting. There the field-testing was carried out with a group of college lecturers. Their positive reactions were very encouraging indeed, suggesting that the approaches used in the Resource Pack could be valuable as the basis of a programme of staff development within a teachers' college or university department. This could lead to a marvellous situation, whereby teacher educators and student teachers are involved together in a programme of collaborative research into the improvement of teaching.

INDIA
N.K. Jangira and Anupam Ahuja

We are both members of staff at the National Council of Educational Research and Training (NCERT) in New Delhi. Following our involvement in the workshop in Harare, we arranged a field tryout of the Resource Pack with pre-service teachers of a District Institute of Education and Training (DIET) in a suburban town. We had twenty-six pre-service teachers who volunteered for this training. The majority of them had completed their twelve years of schooling and were undergoing two-year training for teaching primary classes.

Planning
We had some time constraints since examinations for the pre-service teachers were shortly due. The planning for the programme was done with an aim to maximally orient the student teachers to meet the special needs of children in their classrooms. Care was taken to cover some units from each module. In Units 2.1, 2.5, 4.1 and 4.2 from the pack special attention was focused on *Indianizing* the context. Names of children/teachers and settings were changed to suit our needs. The medium of instruction in the institute was Hindi. Prior to the tryout, selected units were translated and reproduced. The comments in various evaluation reports and the learning journals were written by the student teachers in Hindi. Selected extracts have been translated by the course leaders for reporting purposes.

Before we began our tryout, the Principal of the institute was acquainted with the Resource Pack and asked to communicate and discuss it with the students. The training was spread over a period of three weeks, including three full days and one half day. Unfortunately no follow-up was done after the training because of the approaching examinations. All sessions were taken during normal working hours.

Sufficient time was made available between sessions in order to read the study material and carry out follow-up exercises in the neighbourhood schools. A staff member of the institution acted as a mediator and co-ordinated these exercises. Units 1.3, 1.4, 3.6, 3.7 and 3.8 had follow-up exercises. The follow-up exercises referred to involved trying out the material and methods learnt in practising schools.

The Process

To begin with, we emphasized the utility and importance of the five learning strategies and demonstrated how they would form a continuous part of the training programme. The sessions were held in a naturally well-lit, spacious room. Participants shared working tables which could be easily moved around for group work. Sessions were from 10.00 am to 5.00 pm on the full days and from 9.00 am to 2.00 pm on the half day.

As a group the teachers appreciated and realized the importance of the five learning strategies recommended in the pack. For example, one student noted:

'From my point of view an education system based on the five principles of learning will prove to be highly useful because, firstly, children will increase their knowledge by active involvement and, secondly, they will be able to solve ordinary problems with mutual consent.'

Participants were introduced to maintaining a learning journal. This was very well-taken and some of them realized that they had never thought about the value of written reflections. Some of their comments illustrate this:

'Probably for the first time in my life, I have written my learning journal and enjoyed it.'

'I have learnt to write our learning journal daily.'

'Writing daily our learning journal is important both for teacher and taught.'

In the beginning of the transaction we made sure that we should work on creating a comfortable rapport and come to first name terms. We were conscious of the fact that this was no small task and would take time – the participants were a student group used to maintaining a distance with their trainers. We kept assuring and motivating them to be open in sharing their thoughts before and during the training. The exchanges in the tea and lunch breaks helped immensely. Though there was initial hesitation, they slowly started participating and appreciating the atmosphere, as is shown by the comments below:

'The way the team spoke and made us learn was highly appreciable.'

'I liked the way the team of NCERT made us interact, understand, encourage and speak to each other.'

'I am very happy that I am working with NCERT as a team and the method used in this programme. I am enjoying how all of us are participating and interacting as old friends with everybody.'

Whilst some student teachers felt that the responses would have been better if we had had more children in the class, the follow-up exercises in local schools were well received. For example, one student teacher remarked:

'The implementation of Units 1.3 and 1.4 was very interesting and appropriate. The most interesting thing coming out was that every child enjoys learning in a different way.'

As the sessions progressed it was observed that student teacher involvement and enthusiasm were growing. For example, on the first day there were doubts regarding writing on flip charts. Questions were raised regarding the format and extent of detailed information to be written. Some groups also faced difficulties in taking everyone's views in the group and listing the thoughts together. Some participants tended to be passive listeners initially. Most of them, however, appreciated the first day itself. They observed:

'I found the course useful and learnt that learning is not to be necessarily from teachers but also from our own end. Secondly, we can learn what we don't know from peers. It was useful to remember that everybody should make it a habit to listen. It helps to increase our knowledge and we learn from our mistakes also.'

'We got an opportunity to discuss individually and in groups during this course. We had both small and large groups. We got an opportunity to express our views and know others' views and experiences. We also did practical work during this period.'

'We did not feel that we were sitting in a training programme. It was more like a group of friends discussing things at home.'

'After today's work, I have become so interested in this course that I will not miss even a single class or period.'

For this group of student teachers, already following a training course for teaching primary classes, integrating the material of the Resource Pack by using the five recommended strategies proved to be quite useful. Though initially it took the group a session to understand the logistics of the approaches used, it soon became very popular. They appreciated involvement in the learning process. The relaxed and free atmosphere also contributed to a large extent.

Various ideas for group formation were tried out. For example, grouping was done on the basis of first names (in alphabetic order), numerals, seasons of the year, alphabets, dress, non-vegetarians, vegetarians, etc.

Interest was sustained because of different methods of group formation and informal discussion on topics of practical interest. Shifting from one topic to another, without losing the central emphasis, helped ease any possibility of stagnation. The following comments express the participants views amply:

'We worked individually, in pairs and in groups. We experienced each others' viewpoints in a group and learning became easy.'

'The style of presenting the units was good. We were first told the aim, the given the material to read and then evaluated it after thinking about it. From this our reasoning power increased.'

'We worked with a lot of co-operation.'

'While reading on our own many questions came to our mind which were also answered. The process of presenting the content is very good.'

'We gained detailed knowledge through mutual discussion.'

Evaluation

Our evaluation data revealed views on improvements needed in the grouping process:

'Sometimes I did not like to work in a group because at times one person may feel inferior to the other person. Again your view may not be shared with the whole group. I found myself in groups when my friends were in another.'

'Once when we had a group of seven members I did not like it as everyone did not get an opportunity to express their views.'

Comments such as these left us thinking that, though working in groups was well taken, had we done full justice to our planning? Were not the sessions spread over only a few days? Though from our end we had provided sufficient time during the sessions for reading and tryout, would the responses have changed had we provided shorter time gaps?

The school visit we arranged for the students also did not work out the way we wanted it to. What happened? Where did we slip-up?

Initially, a visit had been made to the school by us and we were told about the way it functioned. Since the children were not available on that day because of an unscheduled visit by an inspector and early closure, we went by what the authorities told us. However, on visiting the school with the student teachers we found to our dismay that the school was functioning more like a special school than a general school. It was projecting all of what integration should not be. The damage having been done, the only recourse left was to use it as a negative exemplar of integration for discussion. In this way, possibilities of integration were discussed and the students drew their own conclusions.

From our tryout of selected units of the four modules, it became clear that the practical application of the material helped a great deal in developing thinking and enhancing the teaching-practice skills of student teachers. Imparting the content through participation encouraged them to interact and reflect on their own thinking, and inference from discussions was also very useful. The student teachers seemed to have understood and used the principles in their classroom practice, basing their work on the content communicated through the material. This also helped them to look closely at the special needs of children and find ways of meeting special needs in the classroom, whilst still following a common curriculum. The content also helped them to visualize their roles as teachers, and the problems that arise and how to handle them, when necessary seeking available support.

We realized as course leaders that this group of pre-service teachers enjoyed the content of the training. They appreciated it in particular because it was practical and they could relate it to their situation. However, while discussing the content it was evident that they had limited practical experience.

The methods of transacting the Resource Pack were instrumental in maintaining a lively interest throughout. In particular the participants liked discussing in groups. Indeed, they proved to be enthusiastic and keen learners, open to different viewpoints. Overall, the training content fitted well with their Diploma in Education programme.

The support and co-operation received from the principal and the rest of the faculty of the institute was our great strength. The presence of the principal and the lecturers during the sessions helped to build the climate of learning together.

Conclusion

Pre-service teachers, if convinced and involved, can develop their teaching approaches. A number of other pre-service teachers who had not volunteered for this training at the beginning wanted similar training to be organized for them. Such requests also came from their principal and senior teachers. This helped us realize the usefulness of the content of the course for them too. Even those pre-service teachers who attended the training wanted it to be of a longer duration.

Our evaluation of the various data obtained from the student teachers shows their gains and change in outlook. The group seemed to be convinced of the advantages of educating children with special needs within a common curriculum in the ordinary schools. We will conclude with some extracts that illustrate this point:

> 'We learnt that all children are special and about the methods by which we can teach them.'

'The whole course was interesting. We were given knowledge about many facts. This attitude that children with special needs cannot be taught with normal children changed. I liked the child-to-child approach and co-operative learning system and found them more practical.'

'The most important thing which I felt is that special children should be given an opportunity to study with general children.'

'The important thing which stood out was that special children must be educated with the normal children in general school so that they can also progress like normal children and not develop any inferiority complex.'

KENYA
Sophia Ngaywa and Grace Wang'ombe

The field-testing of the Resource Pack in Kenya was carried out at Highridge Teachers' College in Nairobi. We are both lecturers in the College. Our work involved us in using the pack with a group of student teachers who in turn tried out the recommended approaches in local primary schools as part of their teaching practice.

There were sixteen participants, nine men and seven women. These participants were pre-service resident students. They were randomly selected from the six classes of second year students at Highridge Teachers' College. The majority had taught as untrained teachers prior to being admitted to the college, with two to six years teaching practice.

Methods
A variety of methods was used during the sessions. The participants were arranged in groups which occasionally changed in terms of size. Participants were also given tasks which they carried out in their various groups and at times on their own. We encouraged the participants to interact as much as possible and to present any problems that they were experiencing in their classes. These problems were discussed during the review of the day and at times before the session started. Solutions to the problems were discussed and participants were left to decide which solution was best for their particular problem.

The participants were generally of the same level. However, as would be expected, a few participants could easily have dominated the discussions had we not been alert.

Throughout the sessions participants were actively involved and they were very interested. When the sessions were used for problem-solving, their interest increased. Parts of the pack which brought about discussions relevant to the participants, such as classroom practices, were also very popular, and invoked healthy and sometimes heated discussions.

Some participants experienced difficulties when they were asked to read sections of the pack silently. They were too slow, thereby taking too much time. When asked to read sections of the pack in their own time outside the sessions, some participants did not do so at all. This would then mean that more time had to be taken during the session to cover work which was meant to be covered outside the workshop time.

On the other hand, reading sections of the pack aloud was very well done by the participants and appeared to help them to understand the materials better. They were also eager to participate in reading out loud.

Brainstorming sessions were very interesting and very well received by the participants. When asked to communicate through illustrations, the participants produced diverse illustrations, yet on the same idea.

The use of continued feedback, demonstration and practice were also very successful. Support from fellow participants, especially by way of advice, was particularly valuable. The participants also negotiated the approaches they were going to use in their various classes during the sessions. Then they would inform us of their decisions.

Some difficulties

A difficulty that we experienced resulted from lack of adequate time. We found that the time we had allocated – three and a half hours a day – was not enough. Indeed, the sessions often went on beyond this allocated time.

The field-testing exercise had to fit in with the normal college programme. It was therefore carried out when participants and course leaders were free. This was not always easy given the tight college programme and the limited time available.

Participants occasionally had personal problems which also interfered with the smooth running of the workshop. At times, some of the participants were unwell and therefore missed a session or so. Some of the participants also had a lot of work due to the fact that they were on teaching practice and could not cope with the extra load easily.

There was one instance where a participant did not fit in with any of the groups. The other participants felt that he was wasting their time. He had difficulty in presenting his ideas to the rest of the participants. He wanted to base all his reasoning on his own personal experiences instead of considering other possibilities. However, with time, the other participants accepted him as he was. We also managed to help him to adjust to the programme. In fact, he eventually did very well during the field-testing exercise in school.

Sometimes participants experienced difficulties in grasping the concepts behind some of the information in the pack, the negotiation of objectives in Module 1 for example. Some participants did not understand it at first and a few did not accept even after they had understood. This may have been due to the fact that they were associating it with a teacher's specific objectives for a lesson. Teachers in Kenya do not usually involve pupils in the negotiation of objectives. Similarly, college students are also not involved in the negotiation of the objectives of the course that they undergo in college.

We also had a problem in convincing the participants to accept the evaluation of the course that comes in Module 1; because they are used to evaluation at the end of any learning process they felt it came too early in the programme.

The process

Learners tended to perform better when they worked in groups. They seemed to feel free and they encouraged each other during the activities. A good example of this was when the participants did the activity on co-operative learning. They performed much better here in groups than individually. It seems that they were able to discover more details in groups than individually. Participants also felt more secure in groups; they were able to talk more freely. This security also seemed to influence their choice of group members.

The sessions were so enjoyable that at times, neither the participants nor the course leaders realized that the time for the session was over. Students are supposed to be in their dormitories at 10.00 pm and the sessions occasionally went on until 11.00 pm.

Participants were relaxed, took part freely and a lot of ideas were shared. This was obviously due to the sheer enjoyment of all involved.

The content was very positively received and the participants felt that it would be used as it was. They felt that if it remained as it was, it would assist the teachers to understand children who need special attention. They also felt that the parents and the community would also accept and assist children with special needs. There was a general agreement that the course would enhance the relationship between children with particular special needs and others. The participants felt that the content on peer tutoring, active involvement, the child-to-child approach, the stories and the additional materials were the most useful parts of the content.

The idea of all people having special needs at one time or another was difficult for the participants to accept at first. Towards the end of the workshop, especially when they were practising what they had learnt, they all seemed to agree with this concept and that they could assist others with special needs.

Classroom applications

The field-testing exercise, where the participants tried out the new teaching methods in local schools, was extremely important. After every trial session, those involved would report their observations to the rest of the group.

Sessions in schools involved arranging or organizing large groups of pupils in small classrooms. This proved a bit of a problem, especially as the participants were sharing classes with other non-participating trainees from the college. Upper-primary lesson periods are about thirty-five minutes each and, time is therefore, very precious and one cannot afford to waste it.

Participants also occasionally battled with the problem of lack of co-operation from some of the qualified teachers in the schools they were practising in. In one case a teacher was unwilling to allow the trainee to rearrange the class for group work.

Some of the children in the schools being used for field-testing had problems adapting to the flexible approaches used in the pack – they were not familiar with such flexibility. A good example of this was shyness in reporting feelings during group reporting sessions. Participants were also apprehensive about the ability of the children to work together comfortably with these new methods.

A few college tutors did not give the participants an easy time either. These tutors were not very familiar with the programme and were, therefore, at a loss when they were confronted with new teaching methods by their students.

Participants felt that the large classes they were teaching and the small rooms that they had were a problem. This was especially evident when it came to rearranging the class for certain group activities. This took too long because the class was overcrowded and, at the same time, the furniture was often inadequate.

The participants felt that the field-testing exercise in schools held professional benefits for them, including feelings of stimulation and wanting to do more for the pupils in the class.

The variety of teaching methods explored in the pack created awareness in the participants. They were exposed to new and exciting teaching methods which made their classroom practice enjoyable and at times even easier. The participants also saw the extent to which the attitudes of teachers can affect a child both positively and negatively.

One idea that all participants seemed to share was that children with special needs do not need to be isolated. They even felt that the costs of running special education institutions could be lowered if some of the children in these institutions could be integrated in regular schools. There was general agreement that specialists are not always necessary for the well-being of the children in school situations.

The participants felt that the field-testing exercise made them more patient with the children and more aware of how they could help children in the class, especially how to deal with children with certain diseases.

As a result, most participants felt that they had to change their teaching methods for future practice. And, indeed, participants have continued to use the methods that they learnt from the pack, in particular co-operative learning, peer tutoring and collaborative teaching approaches. They also observe the pupils more closely and make fewer snap conclusions about the pupils, particularly those who fail to participate or understand.

Outcomes

Significant changes have also occurred in our own teaching in the college. We now both seek to use variety in our teaching approaches, including a greater emphasis on co-operative learning. Improvement is obvious in terms of the students' achievements and the teaching is more enjoyable when some of these approaches are used. We believe that when we employ these new methods, the teacher trainees pick up some hints for their own practice.

Our involvement in the UNESCO project has created greater awareness as to how much has to be done in this area of special needs. Certainly we found during the field-testing in schools that pupils who would have previously been ignored were now receiving attention and responding well.

We had never thought that group work could be possible with large classes, in different subjects and in any topic. Previously, group work was used in certain subjects and, even then, only in certain topics.

One of the most fundamental realizations was that one could work even with very limited resource materials during group work. We found that a few sheets of paper, one marker etc. went a long way during these group activities. This was evident not just in the workshop sessions but also in the schools where the participants were practising.

Most teachers tend to emphasize academic achievement as the main goal in education and tend therefore to ignore the social and emotional development of the children. The field-testing exercise on the other hand made those involved reexamine their own attitude and, consequently, feel that they should aim at emphasizing education for the improvement of the total person. It is not an attitude that can be changed over night, but rather one that can be changed as a result of listening to other people and observing what can be achieved through having an open mind.

The field-testing exercise has made us re-examine our own practices and feel the need to rededicate ourselves to this career. Inevitably one tends to relax after some time in the field and any means that can encourage rededication cannot possibly be over-emphasized. Since the field-testing we have found that we are more patient in dealing with our student teachers in the classroom situation. We try to avoid instantly dismissing other people's ideas or their lack of understanding.

One final point is worth noting. Some of our colleagues at the college did not understand the project. If there had been more time, we would have liked to involve these colleagues in the workshop, this would have assisted in making them appreciate the project and would have helped to create more support for all of us as we explored new ways of teaching.

ZIMBABWE
Chipo Marira and Mennas Simbisai Machawira

The approach taken to the field-testing of the Resource Pack in Zimbabwe was rather different from that taken by our colleagues in the other countries involved. We chose to work with fifteen teacher educators from different colleges. Their experience in teacher education varied from a few months to ten years. They also represented a variety of subject interests, including art, music, languages and home economics.

Our own professional roles are also different. One of us (Mennas Simbisai Machawira) works in the Ministry of Higher Education, whilst the other (Chipo Marira) is employed in the Faculty of Education at the University of Zimbabwe.

The workshop
Our workshop was held at a hotel 27–30 August and the 18 September 1990. The programme was designed by the course co-ordinators before the workshop. It was, however, discussed with the participants on day one of the workshop during the session on participant objectives. Both co-ordinators and the workshop participants agreed that the programme had a reasonable chance of meeting everyone's objectives. We agreed that the workshop programme should proceed as planned, and that there would be room for modifications as and when the need arose.

As the programme progressed, modifications were made to the time allocation according to the responses to the day's reviews. The time allocation for the following sessions was increased:

- Changing practice
- Changing perspectives on special needs in education
- The needs of teachers.

The room was not large and the tables were too big to shift around. This resulted in a loss of time when organizing group activities. Possibly because of the restrictive furniture, at the end of day two of the workshop we noted that some participants preferred turning to the next person, or tried to hold a group discussion in a row.

The participants were generally familiar with each other – they were all teacher educators from Harare teachers colleges and had worked together at the same college, or in workshops, and/or examining sessions.

We were also familiar to the participants because we are key personnel, servicing teacher education in Zimbabwe in both professional and administrative matters. This familiarity was a good basis for integrating the group. However, we realised from the beginning that our supervisory roles in teacher education could create an authoritative structure and feeling, unnecessary in the workshop. In addition to working towards a free and frank atmosphere through the conduct of the package, we therefore decided to make it clear from the beginning that the workshop was totally divorced from our roles, and that the participants should consider us their colleagues. We emphasized that the participants should be as free and frank as possible. As the workshop progressed, we observed that the participants freely asked us about matters of policy relating to the Ministry of Higher Education and the University of Zimbabwe, and critically analysed these policies without restraint.

Evaluation

Participant perceptions of the general working atmosphere is reflected in their end-of-course evaluations which asked them to identify what they liked about the workshop:

'I also liked the enthusiasm, and friendly atmosphere in which the workshop was carried out.'

'I liked the atmosphere of friendly discussion with room for argument.'

Another participant described the atmosphere as 'give and take'.

There was constant pressure to go through the materials we had set for the workshop, hence some sessions were rushed. Participants also felt this pressure, and this is clearly reflected in their daily and end of course evaluation. For example, from the daily evaluations, a participant wrote:

'could have been more exciting if there was more time.'

In the end of course evaluation, the issue of limited time is one feature some participants did not like, as the following replies to Item 3 of the questionnaire indicate:

'I did not like the speed at which we covered some of the interesting discussion. More time should have been allowed.'

'I did not like the time allocated – rather short, and sometimes we did not round off some discussions favourably.'

'I did not like the pace, it was too tight.'

We found that core material from this package cannot be adequately covered in a minimum of thirty hours. This was a vital element during the field-testing exercise and must be noted at the implementation stage.

Negotiation of objectives and a strategy for evaluation are crucial issues right at the beginning of the course. The objectives of the participants can constantly be referred to as the course progresses, and continuous course evaluation during the course helps co-ordinators to constantly readjust their programme or go back over issues that concerned participants before progressing to the next session.

We used the five strategies recommended by the pack. These were discussed by participants and the course leaders at the beginning of the session. Participant reactions to the approaches used during the workshop were generally positive, as reflected in some of the daily evaluations throughout the course.

On day two of the workshop, some participants had specific comments on processes used by the pack to put across its message. For example, one participant noted that to be able to make meaningful contributions to the group situation, one had to learn the tactics of discussion:

'The second day proceedings proceeded cordially, because every participant was now aware of the tactics of discussions.'

Two participants commented on the process of discussions. One wrote:

'Discussions at each stage were enthusiastically carried out, and members, I included, enjoyed today's debates'

Another noted that the discussions were quite meaningful:

'The group approach is effective.'

End-of-course evaluations reflect that in general the participants thought the methods were effective and appropriate.

Responding to the item that specifically requested information on methods some participants wrote:

'methods were effective.'

'methods were reasonably good, and the organizers had done their homework to prepare for the delivery of information.'

'ideal in that it required active participation by all participants.'

'were varied and kept me motivated.'

'were new to me and yet somehow I did not have to struggle to use them.'

The active involvement strategy stands out clearly in these participant responses. It is interesting to note that although all five approaches were used, only this strategy was singled out clearly. The reasons were not clear to us. Our speculation was that whilst active learning is a familiar learning strategy in education, the low level of awareness in education about the other strategies may have contributed to their obscurity in the minds of the participants. Perhaps we should have targeted specific responses about all these methods, rather than leaving it to the participants to comment on methods in general.

From our own point of view, we found negotiation of objectives and continuous evaluations very useful in determining the course of the programme. Our course leader journal was helpful in this regard. For example, after reviewing the proceedings on day one and particularly noting some participant resistance to the concept of integration, we planned a strategy for dealing with that resistance in the coming sessions.

By day three, one of us was beginning to feel the monotony of group discussion. Participants could easily predict that the next move was group work, even where summary sheets had not been issued to them, and there was concern about this predictable nature of the activities. On the 29 August, during the day's review, we noted that two group evaluations reflected that there was too much discussion. These two groups wrote:

'Strategies – too much discussion'

While one group noted that the discussion in groups was very exciting:

'There has been too much group work, this tended to be boring, and burdensome.'

In end-of-course evaluations two participants had this to say about the strategies:

'methods were a bit monotonous i.e. too much discussion.'

'too much of the same style involving participants in group activities all the time.'

Two participants also felt that the methods were too involving, hence tending to tire them.

'methods were too involving, and tiresome'

'were too involving, and laborious. You had to do something throughout the day.'

Responding to Item 4 in the end-of-course questionnaire, a couple of participants made comments on the general trend of the strategies used by the pack:

> 'did not like too much of the same activities by groups, i.e. read the discussion material, then react in groups at the expense of individual expression.'

> 'did not like the overuse of group discussions'

Our own views on group work were that while it was a very effective way of generating data from the participants themselves, and hence an effective way of learning, the strategy requires very high level use of energy. By the end of the week, we could feel the exhaustion from the workshop.

Summarising our findings with respect to the processes we used, we found that they were very involving. Carried through a non-stop, thirty-hour time period, however, they can be very tiring for participants and co-ordinators, and the possibilities of doing a less thorough job when people are tired cannot be minimized. The implications from that message may be threefold:

- Stagger the workshop so that it is spread over a period of time
- Course materials should include high and low level energy from participants
- There should be a balance between individual and group activity. (It would appear that the course we designed was rather biased towards group activity.)

Overall the five strategies have the capacity to achieve objectives and are an effective way of putting across the message of the pack.

Content

We feel that the content is appropriate for meeting the needs of the classroom teacher as a practitioner, and as a resource base for teacher educators on in-service and pre-service courses. In general, Module 2 seems to be a key area for teacher educators, because the general orientation of the new approach is contained in that module. Module 4 is appropriate for teacher educators in Zimbabwe and the Zimbabwean education system in particular because, in general, the classroom has remained the teacher's domain, and that module suggests that teachers could get help from other sectors of society if they open their doors.

On the other hand, Module 3 contains very familiar material to teacher educators, hence the possibility of participants not showing enthusiasm. If teacher educators are going to benefit from the content of that module, some novel ideas need to be raised to cater for their training needs.

The pack is silent on the costs that may be incurred by adopting this new approach. We were inundated with questions of cost to developing nations, and had to constantly and consistently, remind participants that not all integration would require sophisticated equipment or additional resources. Often a reorganization of the school curricula, administration, policy and attitude change is all that is necessary, we argued. It may be necessary to include a unit on costs, to allay the fears of developing nations and reassure those who tend to think that change only comes with high expenditure.

In response to questioning on the content of the course, some participants made the following comments:

'very appropriate, and suitable'

'it was relevant, and educative.'

'rich with good ideas'

'challenging, and yet meaningful'

To get more reactions from participants on the suitability of the pack contents, for training purposes, we asked participants to comment on the suitability of the pack for three levels of teacher education:

- college lecturers
- pre-service
- in-service.

The general response was that the content of the pack is appropriate for all levels.

In response to whether or not it was necessary to put teacher educators through such workshops, the general response was positive – most felt that for them the pack provided an entirely new concept of looking at special needs. Such workshops would therefore act as staff development, a feature necessary in progressive teacher-education programmes. Teacher educators need to be aware of the content and general philosophy of the pack in order to improve the quality of implementation.

As regards suitability for in-service and pre-service students the participants felt that the content was more appropriate to pre-service students, because the former are likely to resist any change while the latter are likely to try the ideas with no resistance because they do not know any other way of doing it. The second reason was that today's Zimbabwean pre-service student has a higher academic background and would not therefore find the language and concepts difficult. Some participants also noted that if the pack was to be used by in-service students, more content would need to be added in some sections that seemed a little bit sketchy.

Impact of workshop

It was a pleasure to note the gradual change in the attitude of participants from day to day. On day one the evaluations reflected a negative attitude to the whole philosophy of the pack. Some of the strong negative attitudes were as follows:

> 'The whole pack sounded a bit too ambitious. The fact that one is blind, deaf, mentally retarded, etc. is a label on its own, and one cannot run away from it. In as much as integration may be possible, there is no way these children can perform the same way. It would be asking too much from the already overworked teachers.'

> 'I must say I am still for the idea of separate classes for pupils with special needs'

> 'Integration is not feasible'

> 'Very doubtful about the whole thing'

> 'I think it is very well to consider the plight of special children, most of who do not attend school, but to expect teachers to learn to cater

for all sorts of children under one classroom is asking too much. I believe that the special children will still suffer incalculable set backs, while the normal child will continue to benefit more.'

We noted this resistance at the day's review meeting. Having discussed the negative response we had observed, we resolved to plan a systematic strategy to changing these attitudes.

On day two, a participant noted that lack of progress in day one compared with day two was a result of people's resistance to change. Now the evaluations reflected a general melting of the negative ideas of the previous day. Some of those indications are reflected in comments such as those that follow:

'Yes the programme is an ideal one… objectives acceptable.'

'attitudes to disability are changing because of this exercise, and to some degree is an eye opener to certain special needs that have been taken for granted.'

'Our attitudes are changed towards the right direction in that it is possible to integrate on the basis that all children are special'

'my conception of the special needs has broadened, and I am able to appreciate the rationale for integration'

The end-of-course evaluations reflect a major change in attitudes compared to those experienced on the first day of the workshop. No participants indicated that they were still hanging on to their old views. Since it was not possible to carry out a follow-up to the workshop, it was difficult to determine whether there had been a change in practice.

From our experience, we believe that the constant monitoring of attitude change during a course is crucial. A systematic strategy to monitor and counter resistance is necessary. We would also say that the Resource Pack requires implementers who are not only knowledgeable but committed, convinced personnel with unwavering support.

Finally, we have to say that our own attitudes were greatly changed. However, we would be cautious as to attributing that change solely to the workshop we carried out. The earlier international workshop in Harare also played an important role in this attitude change. We now have a total new look to the issue of special needs in education.

One of us (Marira) has integrated most of the teaching styles, namely group organization and active participation, in her teaching at the university. She has noted that her students are fascinated by these strategies and that group work, if properly organized, is a productive and effective teaching and learning strategy. It is intended that two courses for B.Ed. students on general methods for teaching infants, and administration of infant schools, include some modules that relate to the general orientation of the new approach.

The other course leader (Machawira) was able to convince, without difficulty, his superiors of the need to introduce the concept of integration in all primary teachers colleges.

We also think that after the finalization of the pack, we should embark on workshops to initiate teacher educators into this concept.

Of course it is also important to note that our field-testing exercise was carried out in a very conducive environment, since Zimbabwean policy on integration is very positive. The two ministries of education are in agreement on the direction special education should take in Zimbabwe.

Chapter 7

Teacher Development at the In-Service Stage

As we have already stressed, the UNESCO Resource Pack is intended to be used flexibly as part of in-service courses for experienced teachers. In this chapter we present accounts of such courses carried out and reported by members of the international resource team at the field-testing stage. The contexts of these accounts are diverse (Canada, Malta and Spain), as are the working roles of those who participated. Together these accounts give us some strong messages as to how effective in-service courses should be organized.

CANADA
Chris Rose

I am Principal of an elementary school in Kamloops, British Columbia, in the west of Canada. Sometimes I act as a tutor to courses for teachers organised by the University of British Columbia. It was in this latter role that I was able to try out the UNESCO Resource Pack.

The Context
The field-testing exercise was carried out over a three-week period between 3–20 July 1990. Utilization was made of a regular summer school course offered to regular classroom teachers and taught by Steven Lydiatt, an extra-sessional instructor who is Director of Special Services in a School District.

The reason why this contact was made was because of the availability of an established target group of teachers who were meeting during the summer. Also, I felt that Steven Lydiatt's input would be of value as it provided an opportunity for team teaching which would not otherwise have been possible.

Preparation took place during May and June by telephone, and a planned meeting in June. Materials considered useful for reading were gathered and these, together with sections of the Resource Pack, were photocopied for the students registered to take the course. Unfortunately, a problem prevented the material from being available until the end of the first week of lectures which was a major stumbling block during the initial phase of the evaluation.

The participants were teachers registered through the University of British Columbia to take a 1.5 unit course entitled *The Exceptional Child in the Regular Classroom*. The description of this course is: 'A study of learning and behavioural conditions that accompany a wide range of handicapped or gifted children. The emphasis is on accommodating the exceptional child in the regular class through an understanding of the needs and a knowledge of resources' (UBC handbook).

Generally speaking the registrants were teachers returning to university to complete their degrees in education or those going on to complete their fifth year of education.

There were twenty-three participants registered, of whom eleven were teaching at the elementary level in schools around the province. Six were in secondary schools, three in special education roles; two were in special classes; one was a learning assistance teacher; two were completing their fifth year in education; and one had just finished teaching in Japan and expects to be rehired as a Peace Corps teacher.

The course

A team teaching process was used throughout the three weeks although Steven Lydiatt was ultimately responsible for the course since he was the registered instructor. Where possible, the expertise of each instructor was used and, when not directing the activity, the other instructor provided feedback as a member of the group or assisted with the group process.

Operating this way the two instructors were able to model many of the techniques mentioned in the Resource Pack. This process was commented on in a positive way by a number of the participants in their evaluation reports. It also allowed for a natural, relaxed communication process within the room and encouraged the participants to join in the discussion.

The emphasis of active learning throughout the Resource Pack is the major strength in my opinion of this material. The field-testing demonstrated that the units attached to each module provide a wide variety of activities that reinforce the points made in the study material.

Giving participants a say in what they want to learn as well as continuous evaluation were two approaches that also appeared to enhance their learning and provided some feedback for the instructors. The use of a variety of techniques such as video tapes, panel discussions and the utilization of the experience of participants was very successful. The co-operative group discussions and activities reinforced what had been covered.

The overwhelming comment on the questionnaire completed by participants after the course were statements relating to the positive interaction with other people, sharing ideas, thoughts and strategies – in other words, collaborating with ones' peers (seventy-nine per cent).

In answer to the second question, 'I liked…', the majority of respondents mentioned the process – the format of the class, the relaxed atmosphere, the varied presentation using a variety of processes and the lecturers' style of presentation (ninety-eight per cent). Only two mentioned the reading materials. This could have been partly due to the unfortunate delay in getting materials from the UNESCO Resource Pack printed at the beginning of the course.

There is no doubt, however, that the success of any presentation is determined by the level of participation afforded the participants. When information is presented in a dry lecture style there will not be the same degree of satisfaction.

The level of satisfaction and enjoyment was evident throughout the course. The participants answers to the question, 'I felt the methods…' were for the most part positive: 'very good', 'excellent', 'wonderful', 'I looked forward to coming to class', 'very well balanced and made each class stimulating and enjoyable' and 'very versatile'. There were no negative comments which must be taken as a strong indication of enjoyment!

The most successful approaches used during the three-week period were the small group discussions reporting to the whole group and the larger group activities when given a specific job (to come up with useful teaching strategies for students experiencing difficulties for instance). Whole group brainstorming also proved successful.

One technique not used was the use of the written texts collaboratively. This was due to lack of time and because it was felt that the time could be more profitably spent through oral discussion.

Considerable use was made of the overhead projector to generate lists of strategies. The blackboard was used for brainstorming and mapping.

Volunteers were used as members of a panel as well as giving mini lectures where their experiences were seen as unique. These activities proved very successful. The activity was set up ahead of time and participants were given the option to decline.

Simulation activities also proved successful. For example, a walk to the cafeteria as a handicapped person gave the participants an insight into being handicapped and how others might treat them. The initial board meeting to set the scene on integration also proved successful.

The use of video clips of interviews with parents and children with specific health problems were appreciated and useful, and everyone thoroughly enjoyed the interview with a knowledgeable parent, Eleanor McEwen. Given more time, I would have used other panels to stimulate thought and provide other points of view. The straight factual lecture giving research evidence seemed to generate the least interest among participants.

Having the room set up, materials distributed and lessons well planned at the outset each day, resulted in everything running smoothly and the participants therefore at ease. We also experienced the need to vary activities and pace during a three-hour session.

Some outcomes

Giving this course over a three-week period, without an opportunity to evaluate change in individual classrooms, does not allow for any definitive evaluation of changes that have occurred as a result of exposure to the Resource Pack. However, comments on the participant questionnaires demonstrated significant changes in attitude:

'I hope to be a more understanding and therefore a more effective teacher.'

'have a greater awareness of many different aspects of integrating a special needs child.'

'I feel more comfortable and better prepared.'

'I have a better attitude (more positive) towards integration than I had when the school year finished in June.'

'I am much more aware of special needs children and better equipped to handle them.'

'It was reinforced that most students can be integrated and that empathy, acceptance and good teaching strategies will allow for higher levels of active integration and growth for both the handicapped and non-handicapped, irregardless of the medical label for the condition. I am going to try integrating more of my students and stop worrying about having all the answers before stressing to my colleagues that we will learn together (what an important lesson!).'

'through sharing we gain a greater insight and focus.'

'feel more confident about having children integrated into my class.'

'want to share some of the information I've learned with my colleagues.'

'I've really learned a lot in the short time and feel that I will retain so much more because of the manner in which it was presented.'

'Integration can be a wholesome process, and one that I look forward to as a professional challenge.'

'I am feeling more positive about integration. Regular classroom teachers need information that will help alleviate fears.'

'This course has given me more empathy for handicapped students and their parents.'

'I have learned the importance of treating each child as normal and teaching according to their needs. I also feel my perspective on special education has changed. I now see less distinction between all groups of children. I have developed the sense that all children are special and we should teach according to this notion.'

'I feel I have so much more to learn.'

'This course was valuable to me and could benefit other people who are regular classroom teachers.'

'As a result of this course I will be more wary of all students needs – not just special students. All students are special. I will be more wary of the needs for children other than a regular class needs. I will not be so afraid of having one/two in my class.'

The University of British Columbia field-testing was a rewarding experience and confirmed the value of the Resource Pack. Also, through team teaching, it was possible to model many of the strategies, particularly active learning. Comments such as 'I like Steve and Chris, and watching their interactive teaching being modelled' confirmed that we were on the right track.

Conclusion

As we enter a new era in British Columbia, the principles of learning as outlined in the 'Year 2000' policy, focusing as it does on the learner and active participation, whilst recognizing learning styles and rates, and acknowledging that learning is both an individual and a social progress, is complimented by the UNESCO Resource Pack.

As principal of an elementary school, my task will be to ensure that my staff accept this change in a positive light so that all children will benefit. Their in-service training will include some of the exercises from the Resource Pack along with ongoing in-service training in co-operative learning, collaborative teaching and peer coaching.

As a school we will continue to develop the peer helper programme and other activities to enhance the all children's self-esteem. The emphasis on staff development as a means of improving children's learning was a positive outcome of the University of British Columbia's experience. The activities in the Resource Pack provide a solid framework for staff development, although only limited use can be made of them in a thirty-hour time frame. I would like to engage in this activity in the school over a sixty plus hour period and use the five days allotted to staff in-service training plus additional staff meeting time.

MALTA
Charles L. Mifsud and Joseph Mifsud

The field-testing in Malta was carried out as part of the training pro-vided for a newly formed team of support teachers. As lecturers in the Faculty of Education at the University of Malta, our task was to co-ordinate the training of this new support team. We chose to use materials from the UNESCO Resource Pack as the basis of an inten-sive, one-week workshop. This meant that we could provide our par-ticipants with follow-up help as they attempted to implement ideas and approaches developed during the workshop sessions.

The workshop
There were twenty-eight participants in all. The group consisted of twenty-five learning-support teachers from Malta and three learning support teachers from the sister island of Gozo. Most of the partici-pants were middle-aged teachers with long-standing experience in regular mainstream classrooms at primary level and who had received their training at a teacher-training college. Two were recent graduates from the Faculty of Education of the University of Malta, which was established to replace the teacher-training colleges.

Seventeen of these learning-support teachers were recruited at the beginning of 1990 from among regular teachers to provide learning support at Year 3 level (seven-year-olds). The majority are shared between two schools and the service now covers all primary schools within the state school system. They were offered pre-service training and they meet as a group on a monthly basis for professional devel-opment. Currently these learning-support teachers who work in the main with under-achieving children have the following well-defined roles in the primary sector. They provide:

- in-class support;
- individualized attention within withdrawal groups;
- liaison between the school authorities and other support agencies (such as School Psychological Services and the Counselling Unit).

Eight of these teachers joined the service in October 1990; thus the reference in our account to 'new members'. Attempts were also made to involve in the field-testing teachers who are currently teaching in mainstream classrooms. However, it was not possible to get these teachers off timetable because of the shortage of teachers in Malta.

The programme was very intensive and we, the course leaders, and the participants became increasingly tired as the days of the course went by. There was a high level of involvement on the part of all the participants. Certainly we lived fully the experience of the workshop together with the participants. We felt that the easygoing and informal way in which the workshop was conducted helped to create a high spirit of fellowship and openness, and an atmosphere in which the participants were provided with the opportunities to air their opinions and views.

The evaluation data drawn up in groups indicate a number of factors that seemed to encourage participation. These include:

- Active role of the participants
- Variety of methods used
- Clarity of materials
- Sense of solidarity and openness
- Practical orientation of the sessions
- Relevance of materials to the local situation
- Importance given to each individual contribution.

Some comments from individuals which reinforce these considerations are as follows:

'I liked the way each topic was treated. The flow of each session was exceptional, from: "leader's introduction" to "individual reading", to "conversation with a partner", to "small group sessions", and back to the whole group for a concluding follow-up and evaluation session.'

'I felt the methods were very adaptable to our local schools.'

'I liked working in pairs or in small groups.'

'I liked the way the course was run as I had a chance to participate in what was taking place.'

'I felt the methods were very interesting as there was a lot of participation by the course leaders and the participants.'

'I liked the atmosphere present among the participants and the good relationship with the moderators of the course as well as the style in which the course was conducted, i.e. with active, participative grouping.'

'The content of the course was very interesting and relevant to our own situation.'

'As a result of this course I am more ready to speak about my problems with my colleagues and to be open to new ideas.'

'Organizers and participants managed to create an easy atmosphere where every contribution was greatly appreciated.'

A strategy which was highly appreciated by the participants was the fact that they were required to go back home everyday and write down their reactions to the evaluation issues raised in each unit. The participants referred jokingly to this as their daily 'homework'. Initially we were afraid that this would be viewed by the participants as an added burden; however, we were proved wrong by such hardworking teachers. For example:

'The most useful part of the course was its evaluative aspect. This is one thing which we do not usually do very much, at least consciously. But in this course one thing was learnt for sure, that *evaluation* should not be something which is done at the very end, but it should form part of an ongoing process.'

'An important aspect of the programme was the evaluation issues which participants were invited to ponder upon.'

Reactions

Difficulties were encountered initially by some of the participants in adapting to the style of the workshop. The following comments illustrate these reactions:

'Initially it was quite difficult to participate fully, but as the style was repeatedly used we all got involved and participated.'

'At the beginning of the course participants seemed to prefer to listen rather than to discuss. However the healthy dialogue generated during sessions encouraged more involvement from everyone.'

'I felt the methods were very appropriate. I found it a good idea when I heard one of the tutors say: "this is not a normal seminar where you can sit back and listen". I found it good as well that I had to write some sort of evaluation at home.'

The fact that the workshop was based in main on active participation and involvement on the part of the participants was greatly appreciated, as evidenced by the comments in the participant questionnaires. For example:

'I felt the methods were interesting as they kept us all very active.'

'I felt that the methods were very enjoyable since presentation and explanation of materials were very brief and we were given time for discussion (although limited). Sharing of ideas was very interesting and we realized how much we can learn from each other, especially when working in groups.'

'I felt the methods were very successful, and definitely much better than listening to endless lectures.'

A factor which seemed to irritate the majority of the participants was the time available for the various activities. The programme proved to be somewhat ambitious as there was so much ground to cover. The materials generated a lot of interest and long discussions. Obviously the implications of this were that towards the end of the course a few units could not be dealt with fully. Although we had planned to deal with the set number of units as stipulated by UNESCO, it was discovered that because of the richness of the interaction one week was definitely not enough. This resulted in a general feeling of things being rushed, especially where the participants were expected to read through long texts. For example:

'I did not like the way the course was rushed to cover all the material.'

'I did not like reading long texts prior to a discussion as I felt that as time was limited it was impossible to concentrate on such texts. Where texts were in point form, it was easier to concentrate.'

There was a preoccupation throughout the workshop, especially on the part of the newly-appointed support teachers, with wanting to know what was expected of them in their new role. It seems that some of the participants could not make the transfer from the workshop to the school situation and could not appreciate the validity and implications of the course content for their role as support teachers.

'I would have appreciated a practical session in relation to our work as support teachers.'

However, other participants seemed able to make the transfer from the workshop to the school. For example:

'The units were very interesting and related to the work that we do, especially as support teachers.'

'The content of the course was interesting and varied and relative to the difficulties and ideals of supportive teaching.'

Outcomes
Feedback about outcomes was gathered by the following means:

1. Individual and group questionnaires prepared at the end of the workshop.
2. Questionnaires mailed to the participants two weeks after the end of the workshop.
3. Continued interaction with members of the support team during the following year.

Most of the participants registered changes in their attitudes and thinking, especially regarding relatively 'new' ideas like that of team teaching and working with parents as partners. The majority seemed to be very keen on going back to school in order to be provided with an opportunity to try out these 'new' ideas and change 'the rather traditional and conservative set up' of our educational system. Others felt that this workshop had helped them to become more confident and to feel a sense of solidarity with fellow teachers.

However, some participants appreciated that it was too early to see changes in practice and that it was 'going to be quite an uphill struggle to change our local attitudes **vis-à-vis** the contents of this course'. Others clamoured for caution about raising expectations too high:

> 'although we concluded very good ideas we still have to convince ourselves of their validity so that we can start preparing the ground to disseminate them amongst other teachers and to actuate them at our place of work.'

Also some were aware that trying new things out is not easy at first:

> 'I now know that I have to experiment a lot, and try new things out, which would seem difficult at first but will eventually be accepted.'

The majority of the participants felt that such courses should be longer and open to a wider audience:

> 'such courses should be more frequent, spread over a longer period of time, and open to representation of classroom teachers and parents as well.'

There was also a sense of urgency and of missionary zeal for the passing on of what one has acquired from the course.

> 'I hope to try out new methods and pass on the message to the other members of the staff.'

Others felt that such courses have implications on a national basis for the betterment of our education system.

> 'these courses are very beneficial and give an impetus to teachers to bring out any new ideas that might help the all-round improvement of our educational system.'

The strategy adopted throughout the workshop of 'continuous and ongoing evaluation' seems to have left some of the teachers wanting to develop this within their teaching.

'to learn from what I practise and improve on it.'

'the way I am encouraged or discouraged; by way of seeing my progress affects my learning.'

However, what counted most with some of the participants was the spirit of fellowship and support which was generated during the workshop and on which they felt that they could rely for a long time. For example:

'I am now facing my duties with more confidence after finding in the discussions held during the workshop that most of my problems are also being met with by other teachers who are giving support services.'

It seems that the collaborative manner in which the workshop was conducted had the greatest influence on the thinking and practice of the workshop participants. This enabled the participants to see how working in teams and groups can assist in rendering their professional strivings more effective in the long run.

'It was the sharing and collaborative way in which the course in general was conducted that influenced my thinking very much. In small groups people try to contribute more towards the general aim.'

'Group work helped in the sharing of ideas with other members of the whole group. The majority of problems seem to be identical, so most of them have a common solution. Discussing them with my colleagues helped me a lot.'

Finally, it is to be noted that most of the teachers went on to apply their changes in attitude and thinking into their actual teaching practice. For example:

'I found the discussion groups most profitable, with a very healthy exchange of ideas going on. I am using a similar approach in my groups and most of the children respond well.'

'I do practical work instead of just hearing other people talk.'

'I'm now working hand-in-hand with the class teachers. I'm gradually trying to make them realise that if we work as a team it would be more beneficial for the children.'

'I introduced paired reading in some classes and I have asked the pupils to read to their parents'

Indeed, some of the responses we have heard read like lists of New Year resolutions:

'I have started more frequent in-class support and teacher collaboration. I am making an effort to get to know the children's parents and family background more, and I feel more responsibility towards the individual child, e.g. in reading exercises. I am praising children more and preparing adaptable resources in a better way and registering progress.'

SPAIN
Gerardo Echeita and Benigna Sotorrio

The Spanish field-testing was set in the context of a national initiative to integrate pupils with special educational needs into ordinary schools. This initiative began in 1985 (Gortazar 1991). Our work as members of staff of the Centro National de Recursos para la Educación Especial (CNREE) means that we provide support to schools involved in integration activities. Consequently we were able to use the Resource Pack with twenty teachers from ten schools in the province of Madrid. Also involved in this work were advisory colleagues from CNREE and the Centro de Professores (CEP), a local teachers' centre.

The seminar

The Resource Pack was used as the basis of a six-day seminar in September 1990. The participants included six class teachers, nine support teachers, three headteachers and various advisory colleagues. In total there were twenty-seven participants. After the workshop, over a six-month period, we carried out follow-up evaluations in order to judge the impact of our activities.

The development of the seminar succeeded in creating *an atmosphere of participation and active involvement* from the first sessions. Participants accepted the importance of their involvement as an essential step to 'change'; nobody showed a negative attitude or tried to ignore this demand. *Everybody took part*, although there were, of course, significant individual differences.

Participants not only took part and expressed their views when there was a general exchange of ideas but also when working in small groups, although here they did it more clearly and in an active way. Sometimes the general exchange of ideas with the bigger group broke the small group's very active interaction, which was not always restored in the big group session. The importance of small group work was emphasized by all participants, who expressed over and over again that group work *prevented them from 'disconnecting' or not taking part*. This is something that, in the end, everybody considered positive, although a bit 'exhausting' sometimes. Nevertheless, the degree of participation was kept very high until the end.

Participants progressively managed to use different ways of introducing the small group's views and contributions to the big group. The *creativity* of the presentations used increased. For example, in unit 3.4 'Classroom factors', a group presented their choice ('using varied materials') using strips of pictures to which no oral explanation was added; the group that chose 'praising children's efforts' naturally reinforced other groups' contributions and presentations in order to demonstrate their message.

We think that participants considered the approaches followed (that is to say, encouraging active participation, evaluation of the work, having in mind one's own expectations, etc.) as *some other content* of the course and, at the same time, as one of the most relevant aspects of the workshop. We found that they kept on contrasting these approaches with their experience in more traditional and classical-style courses where teachers' involvement may be reduced to a minimum.

Reactions

In our opinion, it was very important that participants never felt *discredited* or criticised because of their practice. Thus they were not on the defensive but, on the contrary, willing to revise their practice, not feeling accused of having, partly or completely, a *traditional approach*. With respect to this, some comments are very revealing:

'The most important thing in this seminar are personal reflections, not so much the content.'

'Methodology is the key to this workshop. It makes you give your whole attention and obliges you to continuously think about and pay attention to the other members' views.'

'I have learnt that if we want to look for and find solutions to our pupils' problems, we have to reflect, because the solution is in ourselves.'

Session atmosphere (encouraging participation, relaxing and entertaining) was very useful to make teachers be willing to get involved in present and future tasks.

'People are excited about the workshop. They are relaxed and see things in a positive way.'

'When you go out, you feel happy and encouraged.'

The most positive aspect of the course might be that participants really had the opportunity to revise their way of thinking and acting; they did not experience it as another 'theoretical course'. At the same time, their anxiety about working with pupils with special needs diminished. One of the participants said:

'We have built the content bit by bit and, to this effect, session development has always been from bottom (pupils) to top (course leaders).'

'Teachers have finished the course feeling less anxious about pupils who are different.'

Everybody could express themselves in their own way but we do not think anybody was 'forced' to do so. The most active people took part more often, but the least active ones also said that they felt at ease. Generally everybody took part at some time or other.

It is difficult to highlight special difficulties about the style of the sessions. Everybody quickly understood what it was about and they gradually became more and more involved and creative. It was not necessary to repeat explanations; a few minutes after they were given, everybody concentrated quite well on the proposed tasks and objectives. It was sometimes necessary and important to intervene in order to help the groups, making unit instructions clearer or ensuring that they focused on the task, and avoiding discussions about other subjects.

Some participants said that they would have preferred more fixed groups during the sessions and not so many changes, although this was not a majority opinion; some others considered these frequent changes a good way to ensure that they remained alert and active most of the time. One of the teachers said:

'I have worked with all my colleagues with the exception of my school colleague. Was it done on purpose? I loved it.'

Big group sessions generally tended to be less fruitful than small group sessions, where participants discussed more. We did not make the most of them until the third day.

There is no need to repeat that sessions were very relaxing and sometimes entertaining. This did not affect the objectives we were aiming at, quite the opposite.

Generally speaking, participants were very appreciative of the contents of the materials from the Resource Pack. They said things like:

'Interesting. They have made me think about a lot of aspects I had forgotten and given me a good share of optimism.'

'Quite complete. They provide a good general picture and especially help you to achieve the *essential thing: trying to change your way of educating*.'

'They meet my needs, reinforce my intuition and practice, and are very useful. They can be largely applied to our teaching practice and allow us to progress.'

With very few exceptions, participants considered the content to be 'real' and suited to their expectations, for it clearly portrayed everyday situations and dealt with difficulties they encountered daily. Bearing in mind the objective of preparing materials that can be used internationally and interculturally, there is no doubt that these views are very important and reassuring.

We did not notice any particular difficulties when participants were dealing with the contents of the materials. A reiterated comment was that 'it was mainly a reminder', things they knew or intuited and partly expected. The novelty was that they felt reassured, could relate different things and apply them to their daily work. Most teachers said explicitly that the seminar had been an *optimism injection* to go on working, the essential thing being that they had revised their educational practice and concepts and *discovered that they did a lot of things well and that they could improve others by analysing their own work*.

Outcomes

In analysing what happened to participants as a result of the course it is necessary to distinguish between:

1. the results observed *during the workshop* and *when it ended*, and
2. the short-term or long-term results obtained as a consequence of the subsequent work done by teachers in their schools. As for these, we can show what teachers said *four months later* in questionnaires they filled in and in a meeting we had in January 1991 with them.

All participants said that the course had helped them to revise their way of thinking and acting. A change in attitude could be clearly seen in some of them, as well as a very positive disposition to face up to the challenge of educating children with special needs. This change was particularly evident in teachers who have begun teaching this kind of children in the present academic year.

Some comments may help to illustrate these conclusions:

'I liked it because it was not a traditional course; I also liked the change of approach, the course leaders being an integral part of the group, including **breakfast and lunch** as something else to create contact among ourselves.'

'I felt reborn to teaching.'

'I have been thinking about changing the approach to my work, especially in relation to my colleagues. I intend to go on thinking while I am working.'

'I have changed some of my views and gone deeply into them; I have adopted key approaches to work that I will bear in mind, approaches which I previously did not know or ignored.'

'I feel able to begin my new job and very excited about it.'

The course methodology was highly appreciated, since it encouraged active involvement on the part of all of those present. It contrasted with the passive role that teachers play in many courses. As a result of this, those participants who are involved in training said that what they had experienced would be very useful for their future training activities.

One of the most significant and noticeable changes was perhaps the *optimism* that participants showed when the course ended, which is essential to start and maintain the changes they will have to cope with in future.

Most of them greatly appreciated the fact that the course had been an excellent opportunity to get to know each other better, to become closer and therefore to realize that they can **help each other more** in their daily work.

They also considered it a very good idea that two people from each school had attended the course and that professional people with different roles had been represented: e.g. headteachers, deputy heads, school advisers, different educational levels, etc. This had offered them the opportunity to reflect about how *to collaborate more* with each other in their work. They also considered it very valuable to have learnt about other participants' experiences.

As for their school practice, many teachers expressed their wish and disposition to *apply* some of the things commented on during the sessions:

- Considering each pupil's individual needs, not only the needs of those who have a 'label'
- Prizing and acknowledging all pupils' work and effort
- Group work and topic work
- Sharing experiences with their colleagues; asking for and giving help.

Four months *after* the completion of the course, the most important lesson we learnt about the workshop results was that it was still having a positive and motivating effect on the participants. Those with teaching responsibilities were trying to apply the things they had learnt to their pupils. Most teachers said that they were more inclined to consider *all* children's needs. The idea of improving *collaboration among teachers and with parents* was also being put into practice.

With regard to their school colleagues and their schools as a whole, all participants said that they were trying to convey to them the main ideas and attitudes learnt in the course, but they were doing it in an indirect and informal way most of the time. Only two teachers (from the same school) had begun to prepare a seminar to be run in their school based on what they had learnt in the workshop. The rest had given up, because they thought they would be considered as 'clever' by their colleagues, who would think they were trying to 'stand out'. These teachers' approach had been to drop new ideas or help some of their colleagues with practical hints but always *indirectly*.

This situation may be peculiar to Spain, for here teachers do not feel motivated to do extra work outside their work timetable and training is considered as a very individual activity, carried out by 'experts', usually in the form of long or short courses.

In this context the materials of the pack had been used as personal reminders of what was experienced in the seminar. The CEP's training adviser's situation was different. She was using a great deal of what she had learnt during the course in her training activities, as well as some of the materials, and she considered them very useful and practical for her work. This point of view was shared by all the teachers who were using them.

These results should make us think about the pack's long-term effectiveness when it is used by individual teachers who are not backed up by their schools or by the majority of the teachers working there.

Reflections on the seminar

As course leaders we felt *at ease* and *confident* with the approaches used and also *very satisfied* with the results obtained. A number of factors contributing to such a reaction should be emphasized.

First, we think we conveyed a message of closeness to the group. That is to say, we never adopted a position of 'we are the experts and you are the learners'. We rather went to the other extreme. In other words, we sacrificed our contributions to reinforce the group's active participation and involvement.

Second, we showed interest in and flexibility towards the group's contributions, whether they were critical to the contents of the materials or not. We conveyed to them the message that their contributions were not only necessary but also important and sometimes very creative and useful.

Third, we showed credibility; that is to say, our contributions and reflections were worthy of consideration and belief. This credibility was partly the logical consequence of our professional position and role, but it mainly derived from our way of working and 'being' during the seminar similar to that of Mel Ainscow in Harare. This leads us to think that it is necessary to complement the pack and its subsequent diffusing approaches with elements and actions aimed to ensure that there are trainers who have assimilated the principles of this project.

It may seem obvious but we also learnt that the structure of the training processes elicited and specified by the pack is exhausting. Since the questions and answers are not predetermined, the course leaders' active involvement is as important as that of the participants', if not more, and naturally the more you get involved the more tired out you are. In a way this may be the biggest difficulty of the course leader's work. This tiredness might lead to lower performance and improvement than expected or to 'losing reflexes'. It may also be the cause of being unable to relate to everybody's contributions, to look for common points, to argue well, to look for adequate examples, etc. In the final version of the pack, in our opinion, these comments on the general approaches should be taken into consideration.

We also learnt that the time devoted to the planning and revision of the sessions and approaches used, or to be used, is profitable and shows up in the results. Improvisation during a session is not to be rejected but it is very important to carefully revise the contents of each unit and to consider which approach is the most appropriate. To do this, the 'peer coaching' approach turned out to be essential. The possibility of incorporating ideas in the pack about 'how to look for, choose and work with another course leader' should be explored.

Making participants' expectations explicit greatly helped everybody (us and them alike) to relate to the contents we were working on and the small change processes that were taking place, to appreciate individual contributions to group work, to respect different ideas, to 'reflect about one's own practice' and to work out new solutions for pupils' eventual difficulties. When the final evaluation of the workshop took place, it was very important for participants to realize that a lot of their expectations had been satisfactorily met. This was also very reassuring for us.

The commitment to a 'continuous evaluation' of what had been learnt in each session was a very new approach for both the participants and for us, the course leaders. Most people considered this interest in evaluation as something very positive and useful in order to achieve the workshop objectives.

In short, our experience in this workshop highlights the crucial importance of all the approaches incorporated in the pack to making teachers revise their way of thinking and acting; hence, the importance of emphasizing their meaning and significance in future developments of the Resource Pack.

In our professional experience we had worked before on these lines (group work, revision of their practice, etc.), but not with the support of simple materials guiding our practice in such a planned and organized way as this pack does. Our materials were the outcome of a more classical and obviously more theoretical design.

It has been very important for us to experience and notice how teachers were able to revise and think about their practice, and learn new things with very simple resources, sharing their thoughts and experiences.

We have seen and felt that what the pack says about training approaches and principles is true – it is not theoretical. This may be the most important result for us.

We are very satisfied to have been able to help a professional group of people to revise their ideas and look for common points in a very optimistic atmosphere which materialized into an enthusiasm that became more and more evident as the week progressed. Participants were very satisfied and regretted that the workshop had to come to an end.

It has also been an important experience for both of us to work together in a training activity. It has been a novelty from a professional point of view and also a challenge. The course organization and co-ordination has been carried out in a complementary way, sharing tasks and responsibilities according to our strongest points.

We think the course preparation and development, which was the most difficult thing to do, has worked well, with a great deal of understanding, co-ordination and mutual support. This has strengthened our positive view on peer coaching. This approach is a success, and should be set up and made explicit with relevant guidelines.

On the other hand, this experience has allowed us to revise our work and participation in the other training programmes we are involved in. This revision concerns: (a) the use of easier more related to teaching experience materials that encourage reflection; and (b) the confirmation of a work practice aimed at listening more to teachers and encouraging them to revise their own professional practice.

Naturally, all this would not have been possible without our learning experience in Harare and the help of the pack, whose content and approaches have been essential to the achieved results.

Conclusion

Considering the results of this field-testing, we think that the project we are involved in can achieve its objectives. The materials of the pack are relevant, clear and easy to use, as well as flexible and adaptable to different situations and cultural contexts; the approach is extremely useful and determinant. However, we fully share Mel's point of view, which was expressed in his evaluation report of the seminar in Harare, that the content is insufficient in itself and creates situations which are very much conditioned by and dependent on, not only the course leader's training experience, knowledge, attitudes and style (the ability to get the best out of each participant) etc., but also on the participants' active involvement.

However, the objectives of the pack will be achieved with great difficulty unless they are accompanied by *demonstration*; that is to say, by a number of actions and programmes to be used in the initial training of the course leaders that will be using the pack later, such as those we experienced ourselves.

It is not easy to lead the sometimes very contradictory thoughts that take place in the sessions. There are 'reasonable doubts' about the pack's effectiveness in a process of self-training, for example, when used by a team of teachers without any external help, especially in the case of not very well-trained and/or motivated teachers.

Chapter 8

School-Based Teacher Development

From the early stages of the UNESCO project we have felt that the most effective use of the Resource Pack would be as part of a whole school review and development initiative. Getting large numbers of staff within a school involved in a series of in-service activities is a powerful strategy for the development of policy and the improvement of practice. Apart from the positive impact of colleagues working in collaboration on common issues, locating such activities in the school overcomes difficulties that often arise when individual teachers attempt to import new ideas and approaches from external courses.

The four accounts in this chapter (from Canada, Chile, India and Jordan) indicate the value of these arguments. All concern staff development activities involving substantial groups of colleagues from particular schools.

It has to be admitted, however, that school-based activities can present particular difficulties. Some of these are of an environmental nature, as in Chile where the physical context and resources were very restricting. Others may be of an organizational nature – local disruptions and interruptions may inhibit the learning of participants; most striking are those in Jordan, where the anticipation of war was an inevitable disruption, and in India, where community unrest led to the closure of schools. In Canada another kind of unusual happening disrupted the programme. A gasoline truck being driven on a winter road over a frozen lake fell through the ice. When water contamination was suspected, the school was closed and a one-day workshop session postponed.

Perhaps the most significant area of difficulty when conducting school-based staff development projects relates to the impact of social relationships within the organization. Unlike courses held off site where individuals can talk freely with colleagues from other schools, on-site initiatives have to take account of existing relationships between colleagues. These may include differences about policy between teachers and management colleagues that come to the surface during such activities. Certainly the account from Canada provides strong indication of the potentially powerful impacts of existing situations within particular schools.

CANADA
Winston Rampaul

This is an account of the field-testing and evaluation carried out by Winston Rampaul (Project Co-ordinator and Course Leader), John Bock (Course Leader) and Val McCorkell (Course Leader) in Manitoba, Canada. John and I are professors in the Faculty of Education at the University of Manitoba; Val is a consultant in a school division.

Cross Lake Community School
Seventeen in-service teachers from one school in the Cross Lake Education Authority, located some eight hundred kilometres north of Winnipeg, were the participants. They received thirty hours of classroom instruction led by the three course leaders mentioned above in five sessions over a three-month period. In addition, forty-five teachers received six hours of instruction during a full-day workshop on principles and forms of learning.

Generally, the feedback was very positive as evidenced in course leaders' journals, the participants evaluative thoughts and completed questionnaires. The reactions of participants have been studied and recommendations have been made about improvements for a group of trainees with similar needs and characteristics. The five principles of learning, and the reflective and constructivist views were highlighted throughout the program presentation as essentials of effective teacher education.

The Cross Lake Community School is operated by an Indian Band. The Band has created an education authority which receives its funding through the Band Council and operates under its jurisdiction. The education authority functions much like a school board might in other settings and is responsible for the curriculum and staff at the school. While the curriculum requirements and staff qualifications are to some extent regulated by provincial guidelines, there is considerable deviation due in part to local priorities but also influenced by the difficulty in attracting staff to remote and isolated communities. These and other factors of a more subjective nature related to cultural values, may in fact have influenced particular outcomes and specific observations.

The school opened in 1987. It has nine hundred and twenty students and fifty-eight staff including one principal, two vice-principals and resource teachers, (industrial arts, home economics, physical education and computer education). The philosophy of the school is to provide education programmes for the mainstream of students, equivalent to those provided in other jurisdictions, but also reflecting the unique needs of the community. Native studies and cultural awareness programmes are also offered to the students.

It is the objective of the authority to staff the school with as many qualified and suitable teachers for this community as circumstances warrant. At the present time sixty-five per cent of the staff are from Cross Lake and thirty-five per cent are non-Indians from Manitoba and other Canadian provinces. The school is overcrowded in that it is accommodating at least one hundred more students than the original capacity for the school, so an addition to the facilities is urgently required.

Participants in the workshops were recruited from this school as volunteers who, after receiving information on the purpose of the project and some details on the range of subjects to be covered, agreed to participate and contribute their own time for a period of thirty hours of professional development spread over five separate weekend workshops. Eighteen participants were initially recruited on this basis. They were supplied with reading materials and course outlines, and collectively selected specific topics to be covered in each of the five sessions. This resulted in a number of modifications and the inclusion of some additional topics.

A needs assessment was carried out through which Cross Lake participants were able to identify the four modules and specific units within those modules which they deemed most appropriate for study. The participants also selected an advisory committee which continued with suggestions and information necessary to customize the programme content on an ongoing basis, in order to help course leaders modify their strategies and tailor them to local needs. In October 1990, in the spirit of *negotiating the objectives* with the participants, the Project Co-ordinator distributed the course outline among the seventeen volunteers and proceeded to give a brief explanation of each unit and the approaches to be used in covering the topics. Following this, participants were permitted to discuss in pairs, and in threes, the course outline with a view to encouraging them to better understand the units and to help them to arrive at a consensus. Then a two-point rating scale was administered requiring individuals, pairs or groups of three to indicate the three units which they considered to be of greatest relevance. The course programme was then finalized.

The course

Throughout the sessions we attempted to emphasize the five approaches emphasized in the Resource Pack. These were in some ways already familiar to many of our participants. Our use of the *active learning* principle, which provided an opportunity for them either to relate their new learning to what they already knew or to solve a problem, was well appreciated. Although they had learned the principle before, they never practised it as a constructivist approach.

The *negotiation of objectives* principle was applied by doing a needs assessment. However, theoretically speaking, we did not apply this in every session. If it meant clarifying our objective and helping group members to become involved in the goal of the session, then we applied it in our sessions. For us, it meant clarifying our goals and helping participants to understand what was coming up next.

Demonstration, practice and feedback as teaching strategies were not new to the participants. However, seeing them demonstrated and being involved experimentally in a teacher education situation was new, valuable and acceptable.

Continuous evaluation as a principle was further reinforced by its frequent application in this workshop. During our sessions we periodically reviewed what we covered. It was easy to do this because we had all our information on transparencies and used the overhead projector to display these as it became necessary. We also wrote down participants' contributions on the blackboard and made reference to their points as the need arose. It should be pointed out that participants found that we requested an excessive amount of feedback and evaluation from them. They asked to be relieved of the group evaluation and we permitted it. Prior to their writing of the evaluation thoughts on individual sessions, we asked them to discuss their views in pairs. In some cases fewer evaluations than the number of persons present were handed in. In my observations of their classes, continuous evaluations, both written and oral, were the norm.

The weakest area of application was *support*. The participants found it much more convenient to be negatively evaluative, i.e. giving strong negative appraisals of learners' products and performances. We repeatedly modelled informative and corrective feedback and positive reinforcers for small increments and efforts with the hope of teaching them. It is quite possible that the habit of being negatively critical is cultural more than a professionally-adopted principle. In my discussions with the principal and the director and in our observations in the staff room, we experienced the participants as being more confrontational than supportive. Perhaps the introduction of more democratic practices in planning and implementing programmes, and more horizontal relationships rather than a hierarchical one with the school authorities, might be helpful in changing a strongly entrenched attitude of negativism.

Opportunities were provided for all participants to clarify their understanding of the content and/or whatever was presented. They were permitted to reframe their own problems and given additional time to reflect upon their practices and those of their colleagues. They discussed issues, vented frustrations and did a lot of thinking individually, in pairs and sometimes in small groups of three.

In the one-day session, the entire staff of forty-five was put into nine sub-groups. Volunteer chairpersons took notes of the small group discussions and made presentations of them to the larger group. They were actively involved in all activities because they perceived the problems and issues as theirs or similar to theirs.

Reflections

Certain factors had an influence on the involvement of the participants. At the beginning, they were reluctant to be open and honest about their true feelings and experiences. As they sensed the trustworthiness of the course leaders, they appeared to open up and spoke about issues as they perceived them. Pre-workshop relationships seemed to affect the smooth operation of the group in the early stages. Some members found it easier to remain silent and let others speak up.

In some cases, when topics were politically laden, some participants preferred to be non-committal. When they were convinced that the information would be treated confidentially, they lashed out at authority figures in an unmerciful manner. Because some participants felt that they were not valued by the community and/or school administration, they did not speak as freely as they could have for fear of reprisal. The group was a mixture of native and non-native, and because of this, words were chosen carefully by some and not so carefully by others. A major factor in encouraging openness was the course leaders' openness, acceptance and unconditional positive regard for the speakers' ideas and feelings.

Our reactions to the approaches used were quite positive. All three of us had some experiences of these approaches, for example, working in pairs and in threes, small group work and discussions were part of our repertoire of strategies. We found them therefore quite valuable, convenient to use and very informative as strategies for studying content.

Certain difficulties did arise when individuals had to express views pertaining to their own thoughts and practices. They did not find it easy to relate to other members with whom they had already had interpersonal conflicts and when issues were sensitive. There was not enough time for reflection and examination of thought processes. For this group, we would have needed at least another ten contact hours in order to cover everything. Funding availability and timing of opportunities are now being examined to mount at least an extra full day to complete the exercise.

The participants were extremely positive toward the style of the sessions. They liked the variety of exercises and the opportunities to voice their opinions, and enjoyed being able to clarify issues and their own understandings. Many of them said that it was their most valuable experience in terms of helping them to think about their own education and their teaching practice. They found the practice of allowing exchange of ideas and the brick wall exercise to be the most valuable aspects of the sessions. They felt somewhat overwhelmed by the magnitude of the problems they face and were not all prepared to accept their own responsibility in what was happening. They felt externally controlled and directed, and that making any change was beyond them.

If people did not do the pre-reading, a serious problem arose. These individuals either introduced their own personal meanings or tried to move the group discussion in a different direction. Another problem was not being able to write all their views down. Some had difficulty just writing what they could say easily. Some did not want to write their negative views of organizational and community practices.

Generally speaking, very positive views were expressed about the sessions. The participants found the methods appropriate and well presented, and they enjoyed the brainstorming. They were particularly motivated because of the informality and the thought-provoking nature of the sessions.

Outcomes

The participants said the course made them think more about the aims and goals of education. They now had some back-up of ideas to deal more effectively with problems. They also liked the different teaching methods we used.

As course leaders, we became convinced that the strategies used were very valuable ones and should be adopted by more teacher educators. The constructivist approach, including reflection, generating real-life situations and examples, 'framing' your own problems and seeking out your own solutions with guidance and direction, has some merits.

The course has made participants:

'think more about the aims and goals of education.'

'have some more back-up ideas for dealing with certain difficult students.'

'feel we can resolve some of the problems that get between us and a good education for the children.'

In addition, participants made the following comments:

'did learn to become a more successful contribution to the school.'

'will use different teaching strategies.'

'really happy to be participant.'

'have more inside information about the needs of the school.'

'feel that I've grown as an individual and as a teacher.'

Our experience did, however, point to difficulties that can arise in conducting school-based staff development projects. As we became more informed about the needs and characteristics of the school, community, teachers, administrators and children in Cross Lake Education Authority, we became convinced that more resources are needed to enable northern isolated communities to meet their educational and development needs. Professionals with a greater degree of appropriate and suitable expertise are needed to solve the most pressing needs of the educators in these communities. The educators there must be convinced that it is their responsibility to accept the challenge rather than operate on the assumption that outsiders will fix things up.

A more open, democratic style of operation may help to put greater responsibility on the educators to initiate change from within. Generally speaking, we felt that the job of improving the educational delivery system in a small community such as Cross Lake needed a more systematic, long-term, programmatic effort rather than one thirty-hour contact project with some hours of classroom visitation, demonstration and feedback.

CHILE
Cynthia Duk Homad and Danielle Van Steenlandt

The field-testing here in Chile was carried out by an extended team of co-ordinators. The members of this team were:

- Cynthia Duk Homad
- Danielle Van Steenlandt – A UNESCO associate expert from Belgium
- Agata Gambardella
- Gerardo Echeita – From the Centro National de Recursos para la Educacion Especial, in Madrid, Spain.

The context
The workshop was held at the Escuela Puerto Rico, a public basic education institution serving approximately five hundred pupils of the Conchali Community, a sector of limited resources of the city of

Santiago. Sessions were carried out in a classroom accommodated for this purpose.

Objectively speaking, it was not an adequate locale; relatively small, cold and somewhat remote. Each participant had a chair and there were four big tables of different shapes which were sometimes used during team work.

However, it should be pointed out that this is the outcome of normal conditions of the infrastructure of this type of public school in Chile, and that the technical division and the municipality even had to make great efforts to obtain this furniture. Notwithstanding, what should be borne in mind is that the physical space was immediately compensated for by the participants' extraordinary zealousness in carrying out the work and by their warmth, so that at no moment did the premises hinder the development of the workshop. The amount of material used (paper, markers, scotch tape, etc.) was only what was absolutely essential.

The participants were eighteen teachers were from regular schools, of which fourteen were head teachers of two neighbouring schools offering education from nursery level to fourth basic grade level; two were heads of the technical units of these schools and two were remedial teachers.

The course

The programme was organized in two separate phases. The first, comprising the 'intensive workshop' phase, was developed from twenty to twenty-five August 1990 in morning shifts from 9 am to 1 pm plus an hour daily for meals. The second phase of 'extensive follow-up' was carried out in five two-hour sessions, held once a week, from 30 August to 2 October.

Developing the course in this way seemed to us interesting as it enabled us to envisage how the material and the process would respond to two different modalities and conditions.

The material did not undergo significant changes other than those proper for the adaptation of the language and the exclusion of some terms of little relevance in this context.

However, some of the activities proposed in the units had to be simplified due to problems of availability of time and because they were found to be too long in comparison to their aim.

By way of introduction, it should be noted that from different perspectives the workshop proved a highly positive and fruitful activity:

- It has provided the opportunity for the teachers of both schools to review and update their thinking with respect to the ways in which they respond to pupils' special education needs. Consequently, they felt confident in introducing changes in their pedagogical practices and accumulated an important amount of optimism in facing difficulties they are aware must be encountered.
- From the project's perspective, and specifically vis-à-vis the materials, the project's validity in achieving its specific objective has been confirmed: 'to help teachers to develop their thinking and practice with respect to the ways in which they respond to pupils' special educational needs'. The materials' strategies, content and design have been evaluated as excellent.
- The experience may contribute to the improvement of some aspects of the pack, along with suggestions for its dissemination.
- From the perspective of the interests of the country itself, the work carried out may serve as a pilot experience of the integration of pupils with special needs, and be very useful within the context of the educational policy of the present Chilean Government, which is aware and responsive to the need for developing this type of initiative.
- It has been a very positive experience of institutional collaboration between the managements of the participating schools, the Division of Education of the Community of Cochali, and the UNESCO Regional Office for Education in Latin America and the Caribbean (OREALC).
- Lastly, it has also been a good experience in terms of personal collaboration among the course's leaders (at first somewhat dubious) and likewise strengthens the positive aspects of the strategies adopted by the director of the project and the enormous possibilities opened up by the use of peer-coaching.

It seems advisable to point out that these results have been achieved in spite of the personal, social and material conditions of the course leaders, participants, country, etc. which are far from being the most appropriate. To this effect, five factors should be borne in mind:

- The country's difficult socioeconomic and political situation
- The insufficient educational resources, both material and human, within the public education system.

- Lack of a clearly-stated education policy and a legal framework favouring the integration of pupils with special needs into the regular school system.
- The difficult personal and material conditions in which teachers of the schools involved in the workshop carry out their work.
- The project's budgetary restrains to compensate for some of the adverse conditions.

However, it should be pointed out that these adverse conditions were somewhat counterbalanced by positive factors which should be kept in mind when assessing the results of the workshop. Among them three should be stressed:

- The vast professionalism, vocation and dedication shown by all participants, stimulated them to find the strength to face the multiple daily difficulties they encountered.
- The decisive support these teachers received from their respective technical units, management and the division of education of their municipality.
- The existence in the country of what might be called a 'spirit of optimism' and a willingness to change and progress at all levels, an essential background for the effective implementation of an education in keeping with the individual needs of each pupil, independent of the personal or social situations defining these needs.

Evaluation

In evaluating the workshop the outlines proposed by the project's Director were followed. After each workshop session the course leaders met in order to elaborate a joint diary to analyse the session's development. We agreed to prepare a common table of contents which should always be followed. The agreed table of contents was as follows:

1. Global assessment of the session.
2. Positive or relevant aspects.
   - with respect to the content
   - with respect to the session's methodology
   - with respect to the participation of those involved
   - with respect to the organisation of the session (time, space, materials, etc.)

- with respect to our co-ordination.
3. Negative aspects and those open to change.
4. Planning of the following session.

We discussed our impressions point by point and took note of the conclusions we deemed relevant and reliable. It should be stressed that this strategy proved to be very positive and useful, as generally each of us perceived what to a certain extent was not noticed by others, reaching a very fruitful complementarily. There was no significant disagreement during these sessions. We paid special attention to the relevance of the units and to the general dynamics produced during the session. As may be noted in the table of contents, we always ended by reviewing our planning for the following day. We distributed the different presentations and units to be developed in the following session, according to our own personal preferences, qualifications and even extent of tiredness or particular moods. There was no disagreement concerning this point and all sessions were carried out as foreseen.

On the other hand, the session of Wednesday 22 August was initiated with an individual open questionnaire distributed to participants. It was structured under the following headings:

1. What is your opinion of the style of the sessions?
2. What do you think of the contents dealt with?
3. What do you think of the materials' design?
4. Other comments.

The session of Friday, 24 August also started with an evaluation activity. This time each participant took turns in completing a sentence according to their personal impressions: 'The most important thing we have learned to date has been…'. This activity was especially rich and important, lasting over an hour-and-a-half, as all participants wished to express their feelings, impressions and reactions to a visit by Raúl who had motor disability and with whom they had carried out a dialogue on Wednesday 22 August in the context of the unit on 'Attitudes to Disability'. At the end of the session of 24 August, participants received the questionnaire included in the pack for completion individually at home, in order to facilitate the group evaluation planned for the final session.

On Saturday 25 August, participants working in small groups agreed on a consensual evaluation based on their individual responses to the standard questionnaire. This proposal was read and commented on by the rest of the participants during the last part of the session, adding the informal evaluation of both course leaders together with the impressions of Mr Rodrigo Vera (OREALC), a non-participant observer at the final session of this phase of the workshop.

It should be pointed out that while reviewing the information gathered through the questionnaires, we observed that it provided valuable issues for the evaluation of the material and process experienced by the teachers. However, this information tended to be of a very general nature and did not supply more specific data which in our opinion would have been important, such as:

- Which were the most relevant contents?
- What other contents do you consider should be included?
- What were the difficulties you encountered during your training?

Given that the responses in general did not take account of the possible effects of the workshop in the pedagogical practice itself, we decided to incorporate an additional questionnaire focused more directly on this aspect. This provided complementary information which we found very useful as regard the objectives of field-testing.

This questionnaire (see below) was completed at the end of the second phase, during the final session of the workshop.

Supplementary Questionnaire

1. What are the implications of the workshop's experience on your pedagogical practice as concerns:
   - Serving children presenting difficulties in your class
   - Attention to the course-group in general
   - Planning of activities
   - Participation in meetings with your colleagues.
2. Among the training strategies proposed in the workshop, which do you consider to be most useful for your practice:

3. Mention some changes you have made in your practice, as a result of the workshop.

4. If you have introduced changes in your practice, do you attribute them, in order of importance to:

   - The theoretical contents of the material
   - The strategies suggested in the workshop
   - The style of the teaching-learning process experienced in the workshop
   - The fact of sharing with your colleagues an upgrading course.

5. Suggestions.

Results of these various evaluations have been taken into account in writing this account.

The process

From the start the group was invited to participate actively. The response was positive because the sessions were increasingly enriched by the frequent statements and contributions of participants in relation to their personal experience.

The dynamics generated due to the implementation of the strategies proposed in the workshop facilitated the rapid involvement of participants in the work. This established a direct relationship between the experience participants' were undergoing and their practice in the classroom, presenting it as an example, reinforcement or comparison of what was being taught. This process achieved one of the main objectives of the workshop and proved of great importance to us (and to the development of the workshop), as it enabled us to associate what was being taught with the participants' own examples relating them to cases which were very familiar. As a result many activities were extremely significant and real for the participants as well as for us.

During the last two sessions there was full, rich and creative participation. When the work of some units was presented to the group ('Classroom Factors – Putting it all together'), several groups opted for role-playing techniques, bringing about an easy going and amusing atmosphere but without losing sight of the need for preciseness in their contributions. At the same time, on several occasions teachers taught themselves, completely dispensing with the help of co-ordinators; this was something we had already experienced during our initial training in Harare.

None of the participants expressed difficulties in involving and hitching on to the individual, peer or group activities proposed. Instructions were understood without difficulty and in a very short time the teachers were able to focus on the tasks.

No significant or worthy-of-mention distractions, delays or misunderstandings occurred, and good use was made of the available time; although sometimes it would have been desirable to attain more, the overall impression was that on this occasion the limited time available was not a major problem.

Several factors contributed to achieving close participation:

- The fact that participants were colleagues from the same schools
- The atmosphere of trust among co-ordinators and the group
- The group's structure (all belonging to the first cycle)
- The methodological style used.

However, in our opinion the decisive factors were as follows:

- Participants had the opportunity to express themselves during several evaluations of the programme
- The material, both in its content and in its proposal, met the real needs of the teaching staff
- The possibility of relating with a disabled person (visit of Raúl Arroyo, with motor disability).

At the start of the workshop the group only observed and a critical attitude prevailed as they had many fears, such as having to submit to long expositive sessions and to a prescription on what a teacher should be. This attitude quickly changed once they realized the sense and active style of the workshop. On Wednesday 22 this attitude and its motivation had totally changed; one of the teachers even said, 'I go to bed with the course in mind'.

The main difficulties arose from the full comprehension of new approaches being presented. Progress was delayed owing to the difficulty in getting rid of traditional conceptions of special education.

However, we believe it was very important that the teaching staff never felt disqualified or criticized due to their practice. This avoided them being 'on guard' and on the contrary they were willing to review their practice without feeling 'accused' because of their traditional approach. Some comments are especially revealing in this respect:

'The workshop has helped me to evaluate myself.'

'We carried out some of our work without believing it was good for the children. It has strengthened our work.'

'To us the course has meant feedback.'

'The strategies of incentives, the co-operative learning... are tools which though known to us, were disregarded... Now we have acquired security and firmness in our discussions, even when confronting local authorities.'

Another aspect which gave rise to difficulties was the overload of working hours, as the teachers kept up their regular working hours at school plus the hours demanded by the course, resulting in tiredness and presumably in a lower performance.

The shared knowledge participants had of their reality made possible their active participation. The idea that this pack may be of use to teachers of the same centre within the framework of what may be called 'in-service training at one's own centre' is reinforced by the experience of this workshop.

Sessions were characterised by a pleasant, relaxed and frequently amusing atmosphere. Many persons showed great enthusiasm in attending each day. It should be stressed that friendly relations increased among colleagues of the same school and the collaboration of both schools improved as well.

Some outcomes

Perhaps the most positive aspect is that teachers have really had the opportunity to review their own way of thinking and acting and that they have not seen it as 'another theoretical course'. One of the participants stated: 'This course has no contents, and so enables us to learn how to reflect'. What was stated and commented on was quickly viewed in relation to what they had done the day before or what they would try to do the next day. There were many cases in which several teachers provided examples of how they had applied in the classroom certain ideas discussed that same day, and how they planned in future to encourage greater participation from their pupils, just as they themselves were participating in the workshop.

It is not easy to earmark a certain type of difficulty in relation to the sessions' style. In a short time all participants understood well what was being proposed and gradually became increasingly involved and creative, to such an extent that during the final session the course leaders were almost unnecessary.

In completing the evaluation questionnaire, participants referred to the style as dynamic, responsive, interesting, participatory, integratory, flexible, untraditional.

We, the course leaders, feel comfortable with the strategies used and at the same time very pleased and satisfied with the results achieved as an outcome of them. Although we consider that the success is due to the combination and conjunction of strategies, we observed special acceptance and recognition of the co-operative work implemented.

We did not face major problems along the programme; however, sometimes work was hindered or affected because discussions focused on what the teachers detect as the major obstacle in implementing the new approaches proposed – the deficiencies of the Chilean education system.

An important learning aspect as concerns co-ordination was the proof of the effectiveness of the analysis and reflection as a means for change in the pedagogical practice and of the efficacy of team work as strategy which makes available both the experience and the contributions and support among the members of the group.

In general terms we believe the contents of the material are in keeping with the objectives of the programme and have the great advantage of being very flexible and varied, thus allowing their use in various forms and situations.

Our experience in Harare as students, and in Chile as course leaders enabled us to understand the main role played by the course leaders in order to achieve the objectives of the 'Pack'. The participation of a course leader capable of bringing about reflection and action processes in those involved, as well as of analysing and relating their discussions and contributions, is fundamental in maintaining the meaning of the proposal of the course. In this respect we think that the handling of the material by untrained persons would endanger adequate understanding and use.

Final thought
So our account concludes with a happy ending to a story which began one day in a remote country. A Jordanian woman told an Englishman and then a Belgian about a Spaniard and a Chilean woman trying to implement in a small community called Conchali, a project devised years before which aims at having all students educated according to their individual needs. It sounds like a story, but nevertheless it is real.

JORDAN
Hala T. Ibrahim and Zuhair A. Zakaria

We carried out our field-testing at the Amman National School. Hala is a consultant at ANS, whilst Zuhair works in the Ministry of Education.

In order to prepare for the workshop, we did the following:

- Reviewed the content of the Harare workshop
- Read and discussed the articles provided by UNESCO and our colleagues
- Had a meeting with officials from the Ministry of Education to inform them of and involve them in this project
- Interviewed and selected the participants
- Prepared the workshop programme

The workshop
On a hot, sunny day in August 1990, twenty-one teachers gathered at the Amman National School to attend the workshop. The group consisted of eleven teachers from the school we were meeting at and ten teachers from five different government schools. Their teaching experience ranged from a minimum of two years to over twenty.

We were really faced with two diametrically opposed groups from whichever way one looked at them:

- All the Amman National School teachers are university gradu- ates whereas the government school teachers, except for one, have either two years training at a teachers' college or are high school graduates with in-service training.

- They work in very different environments. The government school teachers work in overcrowded classes of forty to fifty students, with little freedom and no time to make any alterations to the official curriculum and with very little, if any, support from their administration. The Amman National School teachers work in one of the more progressive schools in Jordan, in classes of twenty-five to thirty students, with a supportive administration which encourages the enrichment of the official curriculum.

- It was obvious they came from very different cultural and socio-economic backgrounds. This was mainly reflected by the way they dressed, the government school teachers being more conservative and traditional in their attire than the Amman National School teachers.

The bulk of the workshop was carried out during five days in mid-August just before the new school year started. It took place in a cool and spacious classroom. Every two teachers shared a table. They were easy to move around which facilitated group work. We had arranged the tables in the shape of a U for the opening session and as we expected, the two groups of teachers sat separately on each side of the U.

We met from 8.30 am till 1.00 pm. We broke up the day into three ninety-minute sessions, with two fifteen-minute breaks. We had originally planned for thirty-minute breaks but the participants all preferred to finish early so break time was reduced. At the end of each day, we gave them time to write in their *personal* diaries, which we provided them with. There was also time for either a *written* group evaluation or an oral evaluation done in the form of a round, as described in the Course Leader's Guide. This was all done based upon suggestions they came up with during our first day's activities. We handed out study materials a day before we used them in the programme.

We also had a brief meeting in June, as well as two days at the end of September and a final feedback session at the end of November.

Interactions
As for the interaction of the participants, we were really faced with a difficult task to help the participants break down the barriers between

them and reach a level of smooth interaction. On the first day, one of the Amman National School teachers whispered to one of us that the seating arrangement was not good and they should be mixed up. Little did she know what was in store for them!

We had to make the *random grouping* each time group work was needed, because the teachers always clustered around each other according to their original groups. Even when the tables were arranged for group work in the morning they still did not mix together. On the fifth day, finally, a few teachers from each group sat amongst the other group, but we felt it was not sufficient and continued to do the random mixing. They never felt that the rearranging was imposed.

Although on their own the two groups of teachers did not mix in their seating arrangements, some of the social barriers did break down. On the first day when presentations were made, all those who presented were Amman National School teachers. From the second day, a few government school teachers started to present and this continued and increased throughout the five days. We also noted that during the breaks the teachers started to chat with each other. By the third day they were sharing their sweets, discussing personal and social matters, and most of all, the topic of the time, the upcoming war.

It is noteworthy to mention that the atmosphere between them became informal and congenial. They were open to each other's comments and were keen to keep a cheerful tone throughout the sessions. From the second day they would encourage each other during presentations and would clap at the end of them. If no clapping occurred, they would jokingly remind each other for their share of the applause.

Not only did a co-operative spirit generate amongst them, but also a supportive one. An indication of this was the behaviour of one government school teacher who would never speak up in front of the others and who rarely gave an opinion even in the small groups. This raised the concern of some of the other teachers. On the fourth day, to everyone's surprise, she got up and made a presentation. Throughout, she was looking at one of us rather than the whole group for support, but she really got a strong hand of applause when she finished. Another indication of the supportive atmosphere was on the final day when we did the mountain exercise. We had many teachers from both groups who were very willing to share their personal goals with the others.

Certain factors that did not facilitate the interaction between the groups should be mentioned:

1. Not only the teachers were divided into two groups, but one group consisted of eleven teachers from one school whereas the other group came from five different schools. The Amman National School teachers had their own subgroups and, when mixing of participants took place, one could see them looking at each other to see if they were going to be with each other.

2. One sensed that the Amman National School teachers were on firmer ground because they were in their own school. The government school teachers at times seemed intimidated by it and often commented that they did not have the facilities that the Amman National School teachers enjoyed and thus could not always apply some of the ideas being presented: 'It is difficult to apply the ideas of the workshop in government schools due to the large number of students, the pressure of work and the lack of materials.' At times, meetings would be disrupted by Amman National School teachers being called up to the administration. Fortunately this did not occur too often.

3. The two groups of teachers came from very different sociocultural backgrounds. One day some of the government school teachers criticised the attire of the Amman National School teachers who wore jeans to work. No issue was made of this but some teachers took it to heart. While we were watching a video from Spain two months later, one of the Amman National School teachers said out loud: 'Look! Even teachers in Spain wear jeans to work.'

4. The Amman National School teachers, due to their educational backgrounds and their work environment, were quite outspoken and voiced their opinions with confidence. They were able to draw on their experiences and reach their own conclusions more easily than the government school teachers.

5. The Amman National School teachers were somewhat more receptive to the idea of dealing with students with special needs as their school had started a special class during the previous school year. Most of them were not directly concerned with it but at least they were familiar with the idea.

6. Finally, breaking up the workshop into one intensive week and then meeting two months later for two days had a negative effect on all. The momentum and spirit developed during the week of August disappeared by November. The natural mixing that happened the last day was gone and we were once again faced with the two distinctive groups. Many teachers also did not like coming back on their day off. They were all tired from the pressure of work during the beginning of the new school year, whereas in August they were on vacation.

Positive factors

In spite of all the factors mentioned above, the atmosphere was very relaxed and there was a high degree of involvement on the part of the participants. Five factors that contributed are described below:

1. Many participants felt that the overall organization of the workshop was one of the factors that influenced their involvement. The timing of the breaks was good and they enjoyed the amount and variety of the refreshments that were provided. They also appreciated the effort to stick to the timetable to the utmost of our abilities.
2. Several mentioned that the execution of the workshop by a well co-ordinated team contributed to the smooth flow of the sessions.
3. The policy of constantly changing groups created a feeling of novelty each session. Also, having them choose a leader and spokesman each time helped to promote better interaction and create a spirit of co-operation and understanding.
4. The variety of methods used, such as lectures, group work, rounds, etc. helped to keep them interested, stimulated and active throughout the five days.
5. Finally, the beginning of the Gulf crisis and the upcoming war was ironically a positive factor. The workshop turned out to be an opportunity for us all to get away from the tension of the situation and from listening to the depressing news.

One of our gut reactions to the course was that it was an exhausting experience. We were really grateful that there were two of us to share the execution of the workshop and the project, as neither of us could have done it alone.

Some of the approaches used that we thought quite successful were:

- Handing out the study materials ahead of time. This was beneficial for good participation in the discussions the following day.
- Setting some ground rules for open discussions and group presentations. During the round on the first day, participants mentioned they were annoyed by the chaos due to side comments and interruptions. The following day, we asked them to set their own rules and they agreed that there should be no interruptions while one was speaking, to wait one's turn and to be brief in presenting group work by giving the main points and not lecturing.
- Meeting together at the end of each day to review and evaluate the day and to go over the next day's programme. This helped us decide on necessary modifications for the next day based on the participants' feedback and contributed to the smooth execution of the programme as each one of us knew exactly what to do.
- Having a motto for the workshop that was related to the five strategies of the pack. It was, by the way, well-received by all:

> 'Tell me, I'll forget
> Show me, I may remember
> But involve me and I'll understand.'
>
> (A Chinese Proverb)

Some difficulties

One of the main difficulties we faced throughout the workshop was not having enough time. Three units per module, with time needed for presentations of the study materials of the modules, discussions, field trips, video and slide showings, and filling evaluation forms was too much to do within thirty hours. It was like a race against time. We were always running behind schedule, sometimes having to cut short activities or discussion. We often could not raise certain points we had prepared. Frequently we wished we could have had the liberty to cancel a few units, but did not do so due to the conditions set for the field-testing.

It may have been a mistake to reduce the break time, even though it was desired by all. There was hardly enough time for us to get ready for the next session and have a cup of tea. This limited our interaction with the participants to the point that we could not even learn all their names.

This also may have contributed to the restlessness of the participants by the end of the last session of each day. The sessions were so intense that they might not have had enough time to unwind in between sessions. It could have also been a factor contributing to our fatigue. As of the second day, our anxiety over the execution of the workshop decreased considerably. However our fatigue started and increased as the days went on, so much so that we did not meet the day with the anticipation of a challenge but a desire to have it end.

The debriefing of the units was sometimes a difficult task. On the second day after Unit 2.1, 'Defining Special Needs', some teachers commented that they wanted to hear our opinions not just those of the groups, as well as some form of summary to wrap up the activity. The difficulty did not lie that much in recapitulating what came up from the groups, but in preplanning relevant points or issues that could serve either as a conclusion to the activity or a point for further reflection.

By the end of the second day, some of the teachers complained that they wanted a change from the same style of group work. For this reason, modifications were made to three units and to the presentation of the study material of Module Three. All the modifications were quite successful except for those to Unit 3.5, 'Classroom Practice'. In it we asked them to do their group presentations in the form of role playing a mini-lesson. To our disappointment, we discovered that the majority of the teachers did not know how to role play and consequently the activity was not as we had expected.

Reflections and outcomes

The whole process of the workshop was an enriching experience for us. We learned how necessary it is to be flexible with our programme and to make alterations on the spot or later based on the feedback of the participants. It became clear to us how beneficial it is to use different methods. It was thrilling to see the participants working actively and enjoying themselves. This convinced us that lectures should always be reduced as much as possible. We found out that it was very valuable to give feedback to the participants concerning the points they made in their daily group evaluations. We tried not to be directive but rather to be as supportive as possible. One way of easing off the pressure of the programme would have been to schedule the videos and the slides at the end of some of the days, rather than leaving them all to one session.

After seeing the difficulties that our participants had in coping with Units 1.1 and 1.2, 'A Policy for Evaluation' and 'What Do You Expect?', we realized that one cannot expect participants to take on the responsibility of their own learning when they have never been asked to do so before without it causing some ambiguity, anxiety or discomfort. We have all been trained as students to take in what the teacher says, to have no say in what she/he decides to teach or in how we are evaluated. Suddenly, we are asked to do so without any preparation for it. It would be interesting to see if a group of participants who have experienced being responsible for their own learning would encounter the same difficulties in deciding on their objectives and means of evaluation as those who have never done it before.

We were very happy and often touched by the reactions of the teachers. We felt that their comments were interesting, constructive, genuine and sincere. The style of the course leaders seemed to be appreciated by most. Not only did they feel that we were well-prepared and convinced of what we presented, but they liked the co-operative spirit between us and the democratic attitude towards them. It is worth mentioning that they are so used to a formal relationship with lecturers during courses that the informality of our interactions had a great effect on them.

They all enjoyed the group work tremendously, to the point that they would moan and groan when a lecture would come up. Those who were dreading five days of lectures were happy to see the days go by so quickly. By the second day, the volume of the group discussions was much louder than the previous day. One could really feel a bustle and that learning was active. They appreciated being able to express their needs, to draw on their experiences, to contribute to finding new solutions and to reach their own conclusions.

As for the outcomes in relation to the participants, there are two sets of feedback given below:

1. Reactions given at the end of the workshop, which was one month after the intensive week and during which schools had started.
2. Reactions given after three months of the intensive week.

They both include changes in thinking and practices. The following quotations will best illustrate what kinds of changes took place according to the first set of feedback:

'I have become a better person.'

'This workshop is good for changing attitudes and ideas.'

'The change has to take place in me first before I expect it in my students.'

'This workshop has increased my self-confidence as a teacher.'

'I would like to see some changes in our curriculum, more flexibility between administrations and teachers, giving students more chances to express themselves and increased parent participation.'

'I feel so guilty for all the neglect and harm I have caused these students.' (At this point another teacher jumped to her defense saying: 'You shouldn't feel guilty because you didn't know about them. But if you neglect them now, then you should feel guilty.')

On Thursday (which is the equivalent of Saturday in the West), 29 November 1990, we held a feedback session. It was in the form of a discussion of ten questions posed by us, based on our personal diaries, and on the comments and evaluation reports of the participants. Before starting the discussion, three volunteered to keep minutes and one to monitor the timing so that the discussion for one question would not exceed seven minutes. It was agreed by all that the time would be extended by four minutes only if three participants asked to do so. Thus the meeting would not last longer than two hours.

Amongst the rich feedback presented in the meeting, the following examples give an indication of some of the ways in which our participants had followed up the workshop:

'I no longer pressure some students to finish their tasks at the same speed as the others.'

'I sometimes reduce the amount of work for those students facing difficulties.'

'I am paying them more individual attention.'

'We told our colleagues all about the workshop.'

'We briefed our administrations.'

It is also worth mentioning the change in one of the teachers. On the first day of the workshop, as soon as the introductions were made, there was a sudden outburst from one of the participants objecting: 'If taking this course means that I have to teach handicapped students, then I want to withdraw immediately'. After we reassured her that this would not occur, she decided to stay. A few days later, when one of the teachers asked her how she felt about students with special needs, she said: 'I don't mind at least trying to help those students in my class, if I can.' During the follow-up session, she mentioned that she no longer neglected these students and felt good if she was able to teach them part of what the rest of the class was doing.

On Thursday, 13 December 1990, the Amman National School teachers organized a four-hour workshop to share their experience with their colleagues. They divided themselves into groups of two, each responsible for one section.

They did an excellent job of highlighting what to them were the most important aspects of the workshop. They did so concisely and effectively considering the little time they had. The interesting and sometimes amusing thing while they were preparing their presentations, was the overwhelming concern of all to keep their colleagues active and not to lecture to them. In the end, they came up with a good mixture of both.

Those attending the workshop enjoyed the activity very much and expressed their desire to study the main topics more in depth. They were impressed by the teachers' convictions and understanding of what they presented to the point that their principal said, 'I am very proud to see such quality of performance from our teachers and our students are lucky to have them. It is obvious that they understand very well the process of learning and are sensitive to the types of problems students may encounter. I hope that in the future more teachers will have the chance to attend such a workshop for the benefit of all our students in Jordan.'

Our thinking and practice

What then of ourselves? What has been the impact on both of us? Participating in the Harare training workshop and in the execution of the field-testing has been a very enriching and rewarding experience. The positive feedback and the impact of the workshop on the teachers made us feel that our efforts were worthwhile. We feel fortunate that we had the opportunity to learn new methods, develop new skills and to review our thinking and practices.

One of the more important gains was in learning to work as a team. There is no doubt in our minds as to the value of teamwork after this experience. It was good to share the responsibility and to have someone with whom to discuss the content, the programme and the outcomes, particularly since it was all so new to us. It was not always an easy thing to do as we both learned that we had to accept each other's views and to make compromises. We realised that an important factor for team work was that both had to be open-minded and flexible. We were both grateful that we were able to get along so well.

The following are some of the more important changes that we underwent in both our thinking and practices:

- One of the difficulties facing integration lies in making teachers aware of their essential role.
- We have become convinced of the definite value of group work as opposed to lectures. We have both used group work in activities we have been involved in since the workshop.
- There is greater acceptance of the fact that the student has ideas worth taking into consideration.
- We realize that change is a process that needs time and this in turn has reduced our frustration level when we do not see quick results. Change also needs support. Now it is clearer why we experience anxiety when faced with decisions concerning students with special needs and setting up new programmes. We need someone with whom to share the responsibility and with whom to discuss issues and from whom to get feedback.

- We have learnt how necessary it is to take time out to reflect on one's practices and goals; this helps one to become more objective about one's work and its results.
- The skills practised and developed in the workshop and in its implementation have helped Zuhair in conducting meetings, committees and workshops.
- As for Hala, the immediate questions that arise while observing a class have become whether the activity could have been done in groupwork or with more involvement of the students, how the students' previous knowledge and experience can be used for the purpose of the activity, and whether groupwork would have helped to reduce some of the behavioural problems observed.

A final thought

Finally, in terms of local circumstances, the anxiety level was high due to the beginning of the Gulf crisis. During the breaks, many discussed the war and whether they had made enough provisions; some were worried that they were not with their children in case an emergency did arise. Inspite of all of this, the workshop was welcomed by all as it provided distraction from the depressing news and involvement in something positive and constructive.

INDIA
N.K. Jangira and Anupam Ahuja

In addition to the field-testing carried out with student teachers (described in Chapter 6) we also incorporated the Resource Pack in a school-based staff development exercise, involving sixteen teachers from an English medium school in Delhi. Of these, five were primary teachers, four secondary teachers and seven special educators. This project was undertaken between 27 October and 30 November 1990.

Arrangements

Initially the tryout was to commence from the month of September, but due to local difficulties that led to school closures it started towards the end of October 1990. With the consent of the teachers and the school director, it was scheduled to be held on Saturdays and Sundays. The coverage of the tryout material of the Resource Pack was planned so as to allow teachers sufficient time during weekdays to read the study material and carry out follow-up activities in their classes. While transacting the modules modifications were made to suit the needs of the teachers. For example, many of them wanted at least one day off so sessions were also rescheduled after school hours on some days.

The arrangement for holding the programme on holidays and after school hours had to be planned in advance because the schools remained closed for a long duration and the pressure of covering courses precluded giving teachers time off for training. Only one working day for a school visit was used during regular school hours. The teachers were provided with a conveyance allowance to reach home after the training.

The programme was conducted in different spacious and comfortable rooms according to the requirements of the sessions. Some changes in the room had to be made to accommodate video recording. Each participant had a separate table and chair which could be easily moved around in order to facilitate reorganization of the groups and create a comfortable and relaxed atmosphere. Each day's programme was written on the blackboard at the beginning of the day and the teachers were given an opportunity to react. On some days the sessions began in the morning and continued till late evening while on other days, the work began in the afternoon and continued till evening. Adjustments were made according to the travel needs of the teachers.

The comfortable physical facilities were helpful in creating a congenial work environment. Throughout the weeks it was very encouraging to see teachers' involvement and participation, despite their heavy daily teaching schedules.

Evaluation
The evaluation data indicate the following as responsible for steady involvement of teachers during transaction:

- Discussion of issues of common concern
- Tasks that encouraged interaction between general teachers and special educators
- A multi-channel interaction and ease of communication during discussion

- An informal, friendly atmosphere and good rapport between the course leaders and the participants
- Opportunities to try out the discussed and learned material in the class as follow-up exercises
- Variety and unpredictability about the mode of forming work groups
- Design of the Pack
- Group discussions and working out common points on the flip charts
- Flexibility in time scheduling according to the needs of the group
- Realization by the group that all children may have special needs
- General teachers' inquisitiveness regarding content, this being their first experience relating to special needs in classroom and other material required for different activities.

Some specific comments indicate the feelings of the participants. For example:

'Initially I did not like the idea of discussing in groups. I just liked to listen to the lectures and to others' thoughts. Slowly, I started discussing with other group members and realized that I was myself enjoying it immensely.'

'First writing your own views, then sharing with one person, then in a group, gives you an opportunity to know more about the topic, and also about one's own and others' thoughts.'

'It [the first day] was a demonstration of how coming to a point and involving everyone is an art. Without knowing and feeling it, we all worked throughout the day and achieved success also.'

'The day's schedule with its content serves as an eye-opener to think whether a teacher teaching general children can really teach the disabled children together effectively and to the benefit of both, and how?'

On the whole, most of the participants felt quite at ease while participating in the activities. They showed active involvement in the sessions. We, however, had a particular concern about the potential difficulties of meeting the needs of both the heterogeneous group of general teachers (primary and secondary) and the special educators. Usually secondary teachers regard themselves as senior to primary teachers, and special educators consider themselves as an alienated group in the school. Some regular teachers doubted their role in learning about handling children with special needs in their class, and some special educators thought they were not getting enough from the workshop.

The strength of the transaction of the Resource Pack was sharing the five strategies of active learning, negotiation of objectives, demonstration, practice and feedback, continuous evaluation and support, and points on evaluating progress. Care was taken to keep them as the basis while discussing the sessions, and each participant was given an opportunity to reason them out. There is considerable evidence from the data that participants were aware of and recognized the strategies during the workshop session. For example:

'It was a healthy feeling to refresh our thoughts on principles of learning and the fact that it is essential for a teacher to be a good listener, share her ideas with children, challenge the idea wherever possible in the right manner, relate the text to day-to-day experience of man and, finally, the fact that learning must be made fun as far as possible rather than making it a monotonous, boring exercise.'

Difficulties

What about the difficulties? Perhaps the most significant was the reaction of the group at the end of the first day. The participants appreciated and enjoyed the approach, but were not at all prepared for it. The following comments from individual teachers are a testimony to how they enjoyed the approach and were taken by surprise too.

'I expected a long, uninteresting lecture-cum-discussion. The last thing I expected was to participate so actively.'

'On entering the room my initial reaction was of a seating arrangement meant for receiving lectures as usual. However, to my utter surprise, within no time it was changed for group work and the environment was totally different. It seemed that the workshop would be educative and informative.'

'This process of sharing knowledge, i.e. forming groups each time in a new way consisting of different members, really gave an opportunity to get to know each other and each others' views. There was no stagnation.'

'The way the message is shared is very interesting, lively and effective.'

'Listening to others when they gave their ideas, sharing your own views in group discussions and concluding as one was very effective.'

'The style of conducting the sessions was new. It was the first time that special-wing and general teachers were sitting together.'

Some strong negative comments were also voiced:

'As a general teacher, I wondered what my instructors meant by the term "children with special needs".'

'The reading material given to us and the discussion that followed also did not help much.'

'I was as blank as I could be. I was wondering how these questions were relevant to a teacher who had never handled a disabled child. On the first day everything went over my head.'

'The expectations of learning and knowing something new were not fully satisfied.'

Positive factors

In spite of these reactions, we were left very happy at the end of the day. We could appreciate the feelings of the teachers as they were very similar to our own at the end of the first day at Harare. It was an expected reaction to a new set of materials and a method of transaction from people unused to this flexible and open type of classroom environment. However, we gave a sigh of relief when we read the reactions at the end of the second day. For example:

'By the end of the session I was quite clear about how the workshop was going to proceed and what was expected from us as learners.'

'By the end of the second day afternoon session I felt that the workshop somehow would be an interesting one and knew that it would shape well.'

'Introduction was impressive, group discussions useful, the workshop seems to be useful today.'

'instead of lectures, a unique and interesting way of teaching and learning in various groups, for example, learning in groups of two, four and a whole group was interesting.'

Another area where adjustment was required was time. After the first day, care was taken to schedule evening time to teachers' travel requirements.

A range of factors were noted as being positive features of the methods used. The following points summarize these:

- Working as a team in the tryout of the Resource Pack was a great help in employing various ways of working, learning and assimilating to bring about further changes.
- Individual exercises helped in understanding, orienting and questioning the material.
- Relating thoughts in pairs was also very useful.
- Brainstorming and sharing views in groups was useful.
- Arriving at a consensus helped in integrating thoughts in a group.
- Using a variety of group sizes was very helpful.
- Varied methods of group formation proved to be very successful.
- The relaxed atmosphere meant that everybody was learning together.
- Feedback provided taking into consideration each one's views was very encouraging.

- Spacing the units of a day over a few more sessions on some days was helpful.
- The participants felt that the friendly, approachable, witty and humorous responses of course leaders helped in creating a relaxed atmosphere.

Almost all participants – except a few special educators – seem to be happy with learning and sharing. The following observations indicate the trend:

'I have learnt a lot on how I can make the students in the classroom more active and find out about their learning styles and likes and dislikes of the classroom, etc.'

'I will go back and put into practice what I have learnt in my classroom teaching.'

'These one and a half days have refreshed my mind.'

'Although yesterday I was not sure of how this training is going to help us in the special class, today I feel that something can emerge which can be successfully implemented in our class.'

'Towards the end of the second day many points emerged which could be used in the special classes for our mentally handicapped children also.'

Despite the doubts raised by quite a number of teachers as to the direction in which the first day proceedings were heading, the comments by teachers show the change by the end of the second day. A teacher remarked, 'At the end of the day all of us dispersed with a thought to put into practice what had been learnt from these two sessions in the real classroom situation in our respective classes.'

Some of the doubts expressed by special educators regarding the relevance of the workshop are probably the result of improper introduction of the purpose of the workshop by the Director, who communicated it as being meant for learning-disabled and mentally-retarded children (concerning identification, needs and curriculum adjustment). A special educator remarked, 'As a special educator I think that the content and the topics selected today are not relevant to us. Practical problems the children face have not been looked into adequately.'

Some final thoughts
The last day was devoted to a winding-up session. The teachers discussed their plans for follow-up exercises with others in groups. Time was given to incorporate suggestions and decide on the nature of support from their colleagues. Teachers were also each asked to state the approximate time period during which they were likely to conduct the follow-up exercises. We had visited these sessions and recorded a few.

In addition
Interviews with teachers were recorded. These were more like informal chit-chat sessions to obtain their views. The teachers liked them and found them fun. One of the teachers put her views as, 'We really enjoyed, talking, conversing and were completely at ease.'

As course leaders, we have the following reflections on this project:

1. We need to ask ourselves, can we work on our method of transaction on the first day to reduce the feeling of discomfort? If so, how?
2. We enjoyed maintaining a course journal regularly. It helped us reflect on each step and make necessary modifications. The teachers also enjoyed maintaining their learning journals and willingly shared them with us.
3. A major breakthrough was in creating a relaxed atmosphere in which all of us were co-learners. The distance that exists between the taught and the teacher was conspicuous by its diminished presence. Each participant felt involved working as a member of a coherent group. Addressing each other by first name, sharing a lunch each day, grouping, taking each participant's personal view each day and incorporating suggestions helped immensely towards this end.
4. The follow-up exercise given to the teachers helped them react, discuss and understand the contents of the Resource Pack.
5. The variety and unpredictability in grouping teachers was very well appreciated. Teachers were asked to divide into groups

using numbers, alphabets, alphabetic order of their surnames, first names, classes they teach, length of hair, their heights, colours of their clothes, jewellery they were wearing, dishes they liked in the lunch we shared and primary and secondary colours.

6. Efforts should be directed at working out an accessible comprehensive list of references which could be used by teachers.

7. The visit to a school with integrated children was very fruitful.

8. It was challenging and great fun to build the five strategies into the Resource Pack. These seemed to apply well to principles of teaching and learning with this group of in-service teachers.

9. Stating the aim of each unit before beginning and allowing teachers to react proved to be a good strategy.

10. We were left wondering whether providing specific questions to the participants in the daily evaluation sheet could have helped them give more specific answers. Going by the heavy daily schedule it would probably have not worked.

11. Provision of the material in loose-leaf form and flexibility helped a great deal. We could thus afford to delete Module 4 and only discussed unit 3.10.

12. We learned as course leaders that listening to views of participants, and making them listen to others, is the key to any successful training.

13. Changes in seating arrangements proved helpful.

14. The teachers' concern about time makes us feel that we should indicate something about the time required by teachers to complete a particular module.

Chapter 9

Supporting Innovation

Over the years of the UNESCO project, we have had to deal with many organizational issues and problems. Maintaining the impetus of a project that involves so many people in different parts of the world presents enormous challenges. Also, since funding has been very limited, it has rarely been possible for those involved to have face-to-face meetings. Consequently most arrangements and consultations have been carried out rather laboriously through the post.

Despite these difficulties we have been remarkably successful in maintaining interest and mobilizing people's efforts. Furthermore, as the project has grown, so the process of dissemination to new countries and people seems to have gained an impetus of its own. It seems, therefore, that it is possible to create effective international communication networks with limited resources.

What then have we learned about organizing a teacher-education project that involves the dissemination of innovatory ideas? What strategies are most powerful in supporting such an initiative?

IMPORTANT CONDITIONS

In this final chapter we outline some recommendations for supporting teacher education innovations based upon the experience of the UNESCO project. These will be particularly important for those readers intending to make use of the Resource Pack. However, like so many of the ideas in this book, we believe that they will be of value to a much wider audience involved in educational innovation, particularly those involving teacher development.

An analysis of the project suggests six conditions that seem to have been significant in supporting the development of the initiative. These are:

1. *Clarity of purpose*. This involves finding ways of getting those involved to share in the evolution of the thinking that informs the project.
2. *The management of change*. Since an innovation requires those involved to acquire new ideas and practices, it is important to help them to deal with the pressures that this can create.
3. *Support*. A strong infrastructure of support is a means of creating a climate for change and a means of ensuring longer term development.
4. *Preparation of personnel*. Since people are at the heart of innovations in educational contexts it is vital to have strong strategies for professional development and learning.
5. *Implementation strategies*. Often educational innovations seem to get left at the classroom door. Consequently, it is essential to have well thought out strategies for implementation.
6. *Evaluation and feedback*. The process of change involves people in making sense of and acting upon new ideas. Progress can be encouraged by reflecting upon what has happened and using the insights gained to improve the initiative.

Let us look in turn at each of these six conditions, drawing upon the experience of the UNESCO project, including some further anecdotal accounts, in order to make more specific recommendations.

Clarity of purpose

As noted in an earlier chapter, a distinction is sometimes made between efficiency and effectiveness (West and Ainscow 1991). Put simply, efficiency is to do with 'doing things right', whereas effectiveness is concerned with 'doing the right things'. Too often educational innovations are lacking in the conceptual clarity that enables those involved to be clear about their purpose (i.e. the 'right things'). Consequently energy is wasted in attempting to work with an approach or materials that are under-conceptualized or even confused as to their purpose.

However, achieving conceptual clarity is often far from easy. Significant changes in education arise as a result of complex social processes. These involve people making sense of one another's ideas and points of view, arguing for their own positions, and attempting to come to some agreement as to what should occur. It is through such struggles that policy comes to be created and individuals choose to adopt particular stances towards these policies (Ainscow and Hart 1992). Consequently, it is important to have planning and decision-making procedures that will facilitate the creation of policies that will be understood and acceptable to all those involved.

Within the UNESCO project we have always attempted to organize matters in ways that maximize participation in the development of the thinking that has informed the initiative. As explained in earlier chapters, extensive efforts were made to consult colleagues in different countries and, wherever possible, plans have been agreed through processes of democratic decision-making. Furthermore, considerable efforts have been made to encourage communication within the project. For example, a project newsletter is published occasionally. This allows those involved to hear about one another's work and share ideas. In addition, colleagues exchange interesting articles and materials that they have developed to support their work with the Resource Pack.

Given all this activity, it is necessary to have some means of maintaining overall co-ordination and ensuring that the momentum is maintained. Within the UNESCO project overall, this has been my role. In carrying this out, however, I have attempted to use the expertise of many others in order to formulate ideas, critique suggestions and develop materials.

It seems, therefore, that co-ordination is a vital role in a development project. Ideally this should be undertaken by a task group involving individuals with a range of expertise. In addition to paying attention to decision-making, communication and co-ordination, we have also made efforts to establish a sense of ownership amongst those involved. In all communications, for example, we constantly make reference to 'our project'. Ownership is also encouraged by delegating decision-making to groups working in particular districts or countries. In this sense the organizational structure for the project can be characterized as a form of loose-tight coupling of the sort referred to in Chapter 1. In other words, teams in particular areas are empowered to take the ideas of the project and use them as they see fit in order to make them relevant to local circumstances.

The design of the Resource Pack is intended to facilitate this type of arrangement. The loose-leaf, modular format encourages those using it to select sections that are relevant and, where appropriate, add further materials of their own. In this way the pack remains dynamic and is capable of responding to particular cultural contexts.

This flexible way of working has already proven its effectiveness in a number of countries. In the same way as we created an international resource team, projects in particular countries that involve the use of the Resource Pack are being built around the creation of various national resource teams (in for instance China, India, Spain and Thailand).

In the following account Chen Yunying of the China Central Institute of Educational Research explains how the thinking of the UNESCO Resource Pack is being incorporated into a national initiative 'Curriculum change in pre-service teacher training programmes for the integration of children with special needs'. This is organized by the State Education Commission of China (Department of Teacher Education).

Teacher Training for Integration in China

Our developments here in China have to be big and long-term. The population is enormous. Initially our aim is to influence the thinking and practice of one thousand teacher training colleges and over ten million primary school teachers. We know this will take many years.

We wish to create a decentralized development, with co-ordinating teams taking responsibility for projects in their own provinces. It will take us at least four to five years to set up teams in each of the thirty provinces.

In the last year we have begun by working with teams from four provinces (Sandong, Darlien, Tengjing and Beijing.) This development is supported by funds from The United Nations Children's Fund (UNICEF).

The work began with a two-week workshop and seminar for the four teams, held in Beijing. Each team consists of four members, as follows:

1. An administrator from the province
2. A researcher
3. A school superintendent or headteacher
4. A curriculum specialist from a teachers' college.

In addition, during the workshop the teams were joined by a group of primary school teachers from the Beijing district. This was to ensure that the discussions always paid attention to the practical concerns of classroom life.

Following this workshop each team is organizing field-testing courses for experienced teachers in their own districts. These courses are to be of fifty hours duration spread over a period of weeks. This will enable the teachers to try out some new approaches in their own schools.

The courses will be carefully evaluated using scales that have been developed for this purpose. These scales will evaluate the impact of the intervention on the following:

1. Teacher's attitudes to children's special needs and integration
2. Teacher job satisfaction
3. Teacher competency.

We are also evaluating the relevance of each section of the Pack.

Following these initial trials we intend that the provincial teams will, in turn, create further teams of resource people to disseminate the thinking at local district level.

Thus gradually each provincial project will adapt and, where necessary, develop new materials from the original UNESCO pack. We also intend to produce local video programmes to support this work. In these ways we will develop approaches and materials that suit the needs and circumstances of each part of China.

This project is very important to the development of education in our country. Although we do have special schools and special classes we have problems of resources. It is simply not possible to build sufficient special facilities or create large groups of specialists. Consequently, integration is the most practical way forward for China.

Our strategy is intended to provide an overall framework for co-ordination and support. Within this framework, the main focus for leadership is being established at the local level in each district. It is a massive enterprise, but we are optimistic that by encouraging teamwork we can be successful.

Chen Yunying

The management of change

There is evidence to suggest that successful innovation involves a combination of pressure and support (Fullan 1991); pressure to encourage participation and effort, and support to enable individuals to cope with the difficulties they experience as they accommodate new ideas. Consequently it makes sense to anticipate difficulties and incorporate support arrangements. It is also helpful to sensitize those involved to the nature of change and the impact it may have.

Change is essentially about learning new ways of thinking and behaving. If you accept that argument, it opens up a very helpful avenue of enquiry; it suggests that in seeking to understand how to handle change, alone or with colleagues, we can get some useful ideas from considering what we already know about learning.

Accepting that change is really about learning has a significant implication. It means that schools should be places where teachers learn from experience in the same way as they intend that their pupils should learn from the tasks and activities in which they are engaged. Indeed, we should go further and suggest that teachers who regard themselves as learners in the classroom are likely to be more successful in facilitating the learning of their pupils. The sensitivity they acquire as a result of reflecting upon their own attempts to learn new ideas or new ways of working is influential in terms of the way they deal with the children in their classes.

If we are talking about the introduction of significant changes, involving the adoption of new ways of thinking and different ways of operating in the classroom, it is important to recognize that this is usually a *process* rather than an *event*. Fundamental ideas do not change in a moment, nor are new approaches implemented at the blinking of an eye. What happens is that a sequence of changes or operations is undergone.

It may be helpful to reflect on a change in which you have taken part. No doubt you can recall particular events, perhaps an introductory meeting to discuss what was to happen, or your first attempt to use some new materials in the class. In order to fully understand the nature of the new approach and to become proficient in its use, however, you are likely to have gone through a period of trial and error, possible confusion, difficulty and occasional elation. Gradually, if the change is successful, the process leads to feelings of greater confidence and personal acceptance. In time the practice and its principles eventually become your own, linked to and integrated with other aspects of your thinking and practice.

Accepting that significant changes in education occur as a process takes us on to the next point. Because it is a process, change takes place over time. In attempting to handle change successfully therefore, we need to be aware of the importance of time, particularly in terms of:

- the need for time to be available to learn about new ideas and practise new skills; and
- the need to recognize that the process of personalizing new ways of working will take time.

Too often in schools teachers are expected to make changes overnight. 'As from Monday we will start using the new maths scheme' or 'In September classes will be mixed ages'. The pressure of unrealistic time scales can create stress, anxiety and negative reactions to what is proposed. It can also mean that little or no opportunity exists to learn more about how to implement the proposed innovation.

Textbooks about management in schools sometimes give the impression that change is a rational business, a series of boxes to be followed along a logical flowchart – establish what you want to do, how you are going to do it, and so on. It all sounds rather appealing and, indeed, some form of framework for planning can be helpful. What we must not lose sight of, however, is the realization that the time-consuming process of learning that we call change is, in practice, often untidy and messy. As individuals seek to relate new ideas and ways of working to their own unique range of personal experiences, preferences and prejudices, they can become distorted, adapted or, indeed, totally converted into a form that is more acceptable. Consequently the original purpose, despite having been presented in a logical and rational form, may come to mean something quite different as a result of its adoption by other people.

It is perhaps because of this messy adoption process surrounding the implementation of change that so many high-profile attempts to introduce changes into education appear to go wrong. Teachers seem to have a remarkable capacity to agree to something, say that they are actually doing it and then do something completely different.

The final point we wish to make in our account of the nature of change in schools is to do with its effects on people. Human beings in general prefer to stay as they are. Making changes requires risk taking, so why bother if it can be avoided; it is so much safer to stay as you are. Furthermore, if you adopt something new then you often have to reject something else, and this can be painful. Asking people to alter their ideas, possibly requiring them to reject aspects of their past practice, has the potential to cause considerable damage.

As a result of these arguments, it is quite usual for change to cause disruption. For example, individuals may become unsettled as they attempt to clarify their ideas or, indeed, deal with the threat that arises as a result of being challenged about their existing practices. Many examples of this type of effect were noted during the field-testing of the UNESCO Resource Pack.

Disruption can also occur at a whole school level when attempts are being made to bring about significant change of policy. From our experience it would seem that such periods of destabilization are probably necessary if significant changes are to occur. However, when they occur they can be rather worrying as we saw in the account of the school-based field-testing in Manitoba.

Clearly, therefore, a badly handled innovation, with unrealistic timescales and poor support systems, is likely to create victims. Attempts to bring about improvements can, unintentionally, cause harm. This is why we have stressed the importance of careful planning of support conditions.

Support

The creation of effective support conditions should begin during the early stages of a project. Careful attention to ensuring that all key people have been consulted and feel able to support what is to happen is a vital element during early preparations. In addition it is important that those who are to be participants have clear expectations as to what is to occur and what they will be expected to do.

Within the UNESCO project a number of countries have established national or regional initiatives based upon the Resource Pack. In the following account Anupam Ahuja and N.K. Jangira describe a countrywide project, based upon the pack, that they are leading in India.

Supporting a Multisite Project in India

Our project began in November 1991 with a training workshop held in Mysore in Southern India. Thirty-three co-ordinators from twenty-two institutions (nine District Institutes of Education and Training, eight Colleges of Education, three Schools and two non-governmental organizations) from different parts of the country attended the workshop. It was a mixed group of six heads of institutions, three school teachers, and twenty-three teacher educators. The selection of participants was done in such a way that two persons from each institution were invited for the training. This was done in order to promote mutual support and collaboration. It also helped in providing procedural and resource support. Some teams consisted of the head of the institution and a teacher educator or teacher, while others were represented by two teachers or teacher educators. In the case of the latter, care was taken to see that the head of the institution was informed about the policy of the Resource Pack material to ensure full support.

The training involved an adaptation of the UNESCO Resource Pack material. This was based upon the feedback from the two earlier international workshops and from the learning experiences gathered from the pilot testing of the Resource Pack in pre- and in-service training in India. Four days were devoted to training the participants for the use of the Resource Pack strategies. This was followed by a day devoted to workshop debriefing and two days of practice and feedback. The last two days were devoted to planning and finalisation of the action research projects to be carried out by each participating organization.

The training sessions helped participants reflect upon their own thinking and practice with respect to ways in which they respond to pupils' special educational needs. They helped participants determine their own learning objectives within the general aim of the course and think about themselves as learners. Sessions also helped in considering integration and its influencing factors. Some sessions allowed rich discussions based on sharing different experiences ways of effective teaching and meeting individual needs in the classroom. The participants were required to reflect on the nature of the support available in their settings and how they could develop a supporting network.

Action research projects for the participating institutions were developed with a view to developing capabilities in teacher educators and institutions to encourage implementation of the innovative material and strategies, and to provide research evidence. The assumption was that these innovations, spread over a year and a half, would become a part of their institutional practice. It was hoped that these institutions would evolve into change agents to reform the teacher-development process, making it responsive to effective teaching of *all* children in the classroom.

Twenty-two sub-studies were planned. Nine institutions planned for in-service situations, five for pre-service, six for both in-service and pre-service, and two planned to work on whole-school approaches.

In order to support these various initiatives in different parts of India, we made the following arrangements:

1. Just after the Mysore Workshop a detailed report was prepared and shared among the participants. This helped in consolidating the experiences. Some institutions revised their strategies, after negotiating with their colleagues and heads of the institution.

2. We sent selected units of the resource material and copies of the course leaders' guide for use in projects.

3. Evaluation instruments (based on five approaches) to help monitor qualitative and quantitative changes in teaching learning behaviour were distributed.

4. 'Additional Guidelines' were provided to help in conducting the training programmes.

5. A nominal financial grant of Rs.3500/($140) was made available to the project states to meet contingent expenses.

6. We corresponded every fortnight, sharing experiences with all of the project sites.

7. A newsletter, *Effective Schools for All*, for promoting interaction among participating states by sharing experiences, was distributed.

8. We interacted personally with team members from project states attending other programmes at NCERT in order to discuss relevant issues.

In addition we held a three-day project review meeting organized to help participating teams share their experiences regarding planning, implementation and problems encountered. This also helped participants share their pre-testing experiences, review evaluation procedures, think and share possible follow-up measures and discuss report-writing format.

This 'Multisite Action Research Project' is turning out to be a successful and reflective approach to teacher development. It is certainly leading us to new insights. We also believe that it is developing insight in the participating teachers and teacher educators. Although the project is yet to be completed, the feedback and reporting has been very positive. In the process, a dozen resource persons who can provide effective training using the Resource Pack strategies and design, and implement similar action research projects, have emerged.

These institutions will be used as resource centres for further work in about two hundred district institutes of education and training during 1993–94. At the same time rich material, well-adapted to a variety of contexts in the country, is being developed. New material applied to the teaching of school and teacher-training syllabuses is a significant contribution.

It is expected that this approach is to be applied to all four hundred district institutes of education and training and make these an integral component of teacher development in nationally and internationally funded basic education for all projects.

N.K. Jangira and Anupam Ahuja

Through procedures of the sort described by our Indian colleagues an effective support infrastructure can be established.

Similar arrangements should also be made when a project is to be established within a school. In this context, we find it helpful to agree a contract that clarifies the expectations of those involved, including the roles of any external consultants that may be taking part. An example of this is provided later in this chapter.

Preparation of personnel

As we have seen, the strength of the UNESCO project has been the work of key individuals who assimilated the perspectives of the Resource Pack and then helped to improve it through their reflective teaching. We believe that the training approaches used with these colleagues, and subsequently with many others, are very effective.

The rationale used in this training is, of course, that of the Resource Pack itself. Training is based upon the five sets of approaches described throughout the book.

In providing such training we have used a number of overall designs, but it is essential to incorporate into the programme the following features:

- The careful choice of appropriate personnel, including the establishment of an understanding of what they will be expected to do as part of the project.
- The establishment of supportive conditions in their local context so that they will not experience too many barriers when they do their work.
- The creation of small teams who will participate in training together and then work collaboratively during the early stages of their experiments with new ways of teaching.

- A training experience that includes demonstrations, explanation of theory, practice and feedback carried out in a supportive environment.

- Fairly immediate attempts to implement the approaches in their own working contexts.

- Back-up support during those early implementation activities through planned links with others who are confident about the approaches being used.

In general there are two overall patterns for this training. In a recent book our Indian colleagues (Jangira and Ahuja 1991) have defined these as follows:

1. *Simultaneous training and transfer designs.* Here the training is spread over a period allowing time to put ideas and practices to use in the actual situation in the workplace. One or more sessions transacting the skills in order to implement a new way of working are followed by the preparation of an action plan for implementation in the institution. The participants use the plan and come back with their personal experiences of its implementation. This sequence of activities is followed with other learning units. For continuous staff development, this design is very suitable. It requires a little more effort and response, but the results are very encouraging. It results in a change in attitude of the participant to teaching and training.

2. *Composite training and transfer designs.* In this design the transfer of learning during the training is envisaged after the completion of the in-service training programme. Most of the in-service training programmes run for a specified period; towards the end action plans for implementation are drawn as a post-training exercise. In-service courses during vacations are of this type.

In the following section Cynthia Duk and Gerardo Echeita describe a very sophisticated training workshop they organized recently in South America.

**Table 9.1 Programme for regional workshop
'Special Needs in the Classroom', Bogota 27 July – 7 August 1992**

	Time	Workshop 1 'Demonstration'				*Seminar I*
First week	08.30	Opening Module 1 Units 1.2 1.5	Module 2 Units 2.1 2.4	Module 3 Units 3.1 3.4	Module 4 Units 4.6 4.4	• Review of the basic principles of the project • Presentation of the national report
	13.00	Lunch	Lunch	Lunch	Lunch	Lunch
	14.30	1.1	2.5	3.6	3.3	• Continuation
		Video 'Being	Evaluation	Video 'Learging	Evaluation	• Preparation –
	17.30	accepted'		Together'		practical stage
		Monday 27/7	Tuesday 28/7	Wednesday 29/7	Thursday 30/7	Friday 31/7

	Time	Workshop 2 'Training' (Practice)				*Seminar II*
Second week	08.30	Module 1 Units 1.2 1.3	Module 2 Units 2.2 2.3	Module 3 Units 3.5 3.7	Module 4 Units 4.1 4.8	Proposed national plans Co-ordination
	13.00	Lunch	Lunch	Lunch	Lunch	Lunch
	14.30	1.4	2.7	3.9	• Evaluation exercise	
		Review Feedback	Review Feedback	Review Feedback	• Review	Continuation
	17.30				• Feedback	
		Monday 3/8	Tuesday 4/8	Wednesday 5/8	Thursday 6/8	Friday 7/8

Co-ordinators: Cynthia Duk and Gerardo Echeita
Participants: Group of local teachers and complete group of trainers

An International Training Workshop

This two-week workshop was carried out for representatives from six countries (i.e. Bolivia, Colombia, Costa Rica, Mexico, Panama and Venezuela). There were two main aims: the first was to continue the process of informing other countries about the main characteristics and goals of UNESCO's Resource Pack (similar activities had been carried out before in Chile, Ecuador, Bolivia and Peru); and the second, to prepare new 'co-ordinators' to use the Resource Pack, in initial or in-service teacher training activities, both in their countries and in the region.

Bearing these aims in mind we designed a programme (see Table 9.1) consisting of the following elements:

1. Demonstration (four days)
    Here our aim was to allow our participants opportunities to experience the Resource Pack and its principles as 'students'.

2. Seminar 1 (one day)
    This was concerned with reviewing the experience of the demonstration. Representatives also explained to one another the main characteristics of their national policies for special education.

3. Practice (four days)
    This was designed to offer at least a minimum opportunity to the national representatives to practise and develop, as 'workshop co-ordinators', the basic principles on the personal and professional skills necessary to do it in an appropriate way.

4. Evaluation and planning (one day)
    Finally the participants evaluated the impact of the two weeks and began planning national initiatives for using the UNESCO pack.

We also arranged for local teachers to join in the workshop sessions in order to ensure the presence of the teacher perspective during our discussions.

Two national representatives were selected (only one could participate from Panama) from the six countries, bearing in mind two criteria: firstly, experience in teacher training (initial or in-service), and knowledge of the special education field; and secondly, to provide administrative and political support to implement on initiatives in their own country.

We selected some units of the pack's four modules for both weeks. For the first week the selection was made based on our experience of what best suited the demonstrative character of the workshop.

For the second week we tried to avoid any repetition (only Unit 1.2 which deals with 'expectations' was used twice), to prevent a *déjà vu* atmosphere and to facilitate knowledge of as many units as possible.

The first week had the characteristics of a demonstration workshop, similar to others developed in this project. We emphasized and took care of:

1. clarifying and reviewing the workshop objective quite often ('To help participants to develop their own thinking and practice') and emphasizing the importance of reflection;

2. making explicit and practising the main principles on which this project is founded (active learning, negotiation of objectives, demonstration, practice and feedback, support, and evaluation);

3. creating a 'relaxed atmosphere', where co-operation and equal opportunities for everyone were possible (important here was the existence of different roles within the group; senior officials, lecturers from universities, local teachers etc.);

4. stressing their roles as 'students' and 'learners' during the workshop in order to allow them to experience for themselves which approaches facilitate learning and which do not.

As regards our own work as co-ordinators during this first week, we organized it by trying to complement our 'styles' and to get a balance of our skills, knowledge and weaknesses. Basically, we worked on one module and three units every day. We held two 'formal' evaluation activities and encouraged participants to complete a learning diary during the week. After the second day it was possible to create a support atmosphere which allowed all the participants to be actively engaged in activities. After that, most people recognized that the workshop had been useful because it facilitated their reflection on the way they understood special educational needs and because, afterwards, they felt themselves more able and willing to deal with them. All of them pointed out a significant change of attitudes with regard to pupils who experience learning difficulties. Through different evaluations they showed us that the Resource Pack was appropriate and relevant for their needs, both from the point of view of contents and training strategies.

Some objectives were in our mind for the first seminar at the end of the demonstration: First, to review again the Resource Pack objectives and principles, and to analyse to what extent the activities, strategies and atmosphere of the workshop were following those objectives and principles; second, to prepare the second week in which they would act as session co-ordinators; and, finally, we estimated that it could be useful to share some basic information about national policies on special education in each country. This helped to facilitate mutual awareness and co-operation among national representatives.

For the purpose of this publication, it seems necessary to point out our decision about the units and modules to be held by each participant in the second week. We tried to allocate similar responsibility (to present at least one module and one or two units) to everyone. We also organized pairs and trios, to let them experience the implications of this collaborative work and, of course, to facilitate mutual support and to diminish 'anxiety'. Finally, we gave everybody those units or modules that, in our opinion, were best suited to their knowledge and understanding. This second workshop was useful and relevant for the new participants (a new group of local teachers and post-graduate students of Bogota University – 'Universidad Pedagógica Nacional') and that was important for us.

Following the design, the second week was like a second demonstration workshop for the new group of local teachers, postgraduate students and those national representatives who were not involved as co-ordinators in each moment. The week was totally developed, managed and evaluated by national representatives. During those four days we acted as 'external observers'. Although it was a quite unusual training activity (some people changed their role from time to time), the work was performed very well. At the end, most people said that it had been a significant and relevant workshop, and that the main objectives had been achieved.

Regarding the objective of preparing 'future co-ordinators', the second week was devoted to reviewing the work done and to offer feedback to session co-ordinators. We tried to analyse as much as possible the different uses of strategies, clarity in presenting the objectives and tasks of units, co-ordinators' and participants' feelings, general atmosphere, time and group work control, and achievements for both participants and co-ordinators.

It was remarkable that feedback was given not only by us, but also by colleagues. They could offer a very nice picture of the process because they had been involved in the group work. Moreover, reflecting upon and learning about necessary training skills for such a workshop was highly valued. These outcomes were possible because of a high degree of 'professionalism' and the existence of a mutual support, nice feeling and cordiality among all of us. (These conditions are, at the same time, the effect of the principles and strategies underlying this project.)

During the second week, national representatives were preparing not only their 'practice', but pre-designing one or several suitable activities to inform others about the project and gain more experience of it on returning to their own countries.

The second seminar day was devoted to making a global evaluation of the strategies, to collecting their opinions and suggestions and to getting to know each national representative initiative. We provided some basic instructions to follow up the use of the Resource Pack (publicity, references, modifications of units or modules, etc.), deadlines to receive their definitive projects, and procedures to receive both our personal and UNESCO's support.

The evaluation we made of this experience in Bogota offers us a very positive result. We think that most of the national representatives now have a solid base to become 'resource persons' for the project, and to be involved in national and regional training activities for this UNESCO project in the future.

Sometimes, without doubt, the work was exhausting, quite repetitive as regards the use of some strategies and the workshop 'format', and very demanding for both national representatives and co-ordinators. Because of that, it is crucial to invest, as much as possible, in a careful selection of the national representatives. Otherwise, this activity could have less impact than we wish and need. In relation to this selection, the most important aspect is not so much their knowledge of special educational needs, but their training skills and, overall, their willingness to envisage the new perspective which this project sustains with regard to the education of pupils with special needs.

Gerardo Echeita and Cynthia Duk

A key issue in the preparation of personnel is the use of the partner-ship-teaching approach, including peer coaching. Our experience is that this is an excellent strategy during the early stages of using the pack. Our colleagues in Jordan, Hala Ibrahim and Zuhair Zakaria, put together the following guidelines based upon their experience of working together during the field-testing exercise.

Some Guidelines for Teaching Together

1. Preparation

   Since our backgrounds and experiences in work were very different, we wanted to be sure that we had a common basis or understanding of the principles of the Resource Pack. We went through two stages in the preparation of the workshop:

(i) We both read thoroughly the course leader's guide and all the extra readings that were sent to us. We met several times to discuss the content of all of these materials. This helped us to gain a better understanding of the trends in the field and of the principles of the pack. But what was more important was that through these discussions we found out what each other's knowledge of the field was and what areas we might need to study more in depth, and it also gave us the chance of finding out how each of us thinks and what some of our strengths and weaknesses were.

(ii) Once we distributed the programme between us and did our preparations, we again met on a regular basis, going through the content of each of the units and the study materials. This was done for two reasons: to discuss the content and make necessary alterations or additions, and to know what the other would be discussing in order to provide better support during discussions with the participants.

2. Execution

At the end of every day of the workshop, Zuhair and I met to discuss how the day had gone: good points, bad points, feedback on each other's presentations and the participants' evaluation of the day. We then would quickly go over the programme of the next day and what each one of us would be doing, taking into consideration the comments of the day. We are sure that this helped in making the flow of the workshop smooth and in conveying a relaxed feeling between the two of us to the participants.

3. Summary

In the light of our experience we would suggest the following guidelines:

(i) Read and discuss thoroughly the course leader's guide and any relevant materials.

(ii) Distribute the units and the study materials as a function of each other's backgrounds, interests and strengths.

(iii) Discuss the content of each other's presentations so that the other team mate will be a good support.

(iv) Define each person's roles and duties throughout the day.

(v) Evaluate on a regular basis the execution of the programme.

(vi) Be ready to accept some criticism and to compromise.

Hala Ibrahim and Zuhair Zakaria

During the early stages of using the Resource Pack it is helpful to provide very specific instructions as to the methods to be used. Below is an example of such instructions developed by Anupam Ahuja and used as part of projects in India and Africa.

Guidelines for Teacher Educators

The following are a few guidelines for your consideration before beginning and during transaction of the units of the UNESCO Resource Pack. Read these along with those stated in the Course Leaders' Guide, already sent to you.

1. Physical arrangements
   The room should have the following:
   (i)   light furniture as far as possible to facilitate group formation
   (ii)   enough space to form groups and move around
   (iii) some tables (lightweight) on the side of the rooms to write on and keep the material
   (iv)   a working table for the course leader's team
   (v)   wall space or boards to put up charts
   (vi)   • working plug points
          • no echo
          • curtains
            (if video recording)
   (vii) comfortable working conditions such as proper ventilation, lighting, etc.
   (viii) a blackboard (preferably large) with white and coloured chalks
   (ix)   an overhead projector, if available, transparencies and transparency pens.

2. Before beginning and during transactions
   (i)   Before beginning a course transaction, obtain a list of participants with their academic and professional experience. This facilitates group formation while transacting various units.
   (ii)   Inform participants that home reading assignments are part of the training workshop.
   (iii) While planning the workshop timetable also plan the distribution of reading material, study material and discussion material.

(iv) Distribute study material of modules (1, 2, 3, 4) before starting the respective units. Course leaders should ensure that the reading load is not too heavy and that the participants co-operate willingly.

(v) Record your own action points for transaction before beginning each unit. This facilitates smooth group work and clarity of instructions. The action points can be recorded on the course leaders' sheet.

(vi) Course leaders should try to use different ways to form groups and make a note of each experience in their course journal.

(vii) Instructions for group work should be provided after participants have settled in their groups.

(viii) When starting the transaction of units, ensure that the seating arrangement has an appropriate style. It should not be in rows. Inaugurations must be brief. Group members around a table in a circle is an arrangement which helps to set the tone for group work.

(ix) Prepare flip charts with the aims of the units and at times the activity patterns. It is helpful to have the following flip charts prior to the transaction of the Resource Pack.

 a) Five principles of the Resource Pack, material regarding:
 • Active learning
 • Negotiation of objectives
 • Demonstration, practice and feedback
 • Continuous evaluation
 • Support.

 b) Active listening in pairs involves:
 • looking at the person who is talking
 • sitting quietly
 • doing nothing else but listening
 • responding naturally with gestures and expressions, making no comments
 • asking questions only if there is a need to clarify a point.

 c) Writing journal
 • ideas that you would like to remember
 • questions that you need to think about
 • ideas to follow-up
 • points to share with colleagues
 • reactions to the sessions.

 d) Conceptual diagrams of each module. Study material, salient points and, if needed, a summary.

(x) During group work clarify instructions. You can also ask some participants to repeat your instructions. It should however be a voluntary attempt. Be alert, and keep eyes, ears and mind open to catch discussion points. This information helps the course leader in the final debriefing. Try to make a mental note of the names of participants. Use them while debriefing and interacting.

(xi) While transacting group work, ask participants to elect new members each time to express thoughts to the whole group. For example, the course leaders could make a subtle statement like: 'we would like to see new faces each time presentations are made'.

(xii) Sometimes, it is useful to have the goal and the key steps with approximate time lines for completing a particular activity on the blackboard/flip chart. This is especially useful if handling a large group.

(xiii) Make a daily plan of things to be done prior to starting the workshop. It helps to ensure that all errands have been taken care of and saves energy during workshop transaction.

(xiv) Encourage participants to keep a learning journal. Course leaders need to keep a track of this. For this, course leaders can start by reading to participants from their own learning journals. Similarly, willing participants can be asked to share their thoughts from their learning journals to take care of initial hesitation.

(xv) Follow-up activities should be decided after transacting each unit. Discuss with participants details of the follow-up exercise and seek their personal modifications. Ask participants to give their own schedule of carrying out the follow-up exercise.

(xvi) If possible, take photographs while transacting the Resource Pack material. Try to catch the follow-up activities with children, methods of grouping, group transactions and participants preparing flip charts etc.

(xvii) During the workshop the course leaders should:
- consult each other
- keep moving around the room while the participants are engaged in discussions
- take part in the discussion with participants.

(xviii) If using unit 2.9 on 'needs of the teachers' it helps to invite (analysis bringing out problems) the head of the institute when the group presentations are being made.

(xix) When handling the pre-service group, have preliminary talks with the principal and the teachers of the institute about the following:
- The rationale of the Resource Pack
- The assurance of their support and co-operation
- The deputation of teacher educators to attend the workshop, assisting their pupils in the follow-up exercises.

3. Stationery

(i) Flip charts (size 90 cm x 60 cm); if this size of paper is not available join sheets of paper to have the required size.

(ii) Thick-edged marking pens for group work; at least four colours for each group.

(iii) Sticking material to put up flip charts such as Sellotape, glue sticks, etc. Ordinary pins can also be used to put up flip charts on curtains etc. in the room.
Note: The sticking material should be tested beforehand.

(iv) Envelopes/file boards for putting the units in day and session order.

(v) File/papers for participants and a notebook for writing learning journals.

Anupam Ahuja

Implementation strategies

As we have noted, many innovations get left at the door of the classroom. Consequently, we need effective strategies that will help teachers to try out new approaches. These implementation strategies are needed for teachers, schools, and teacher educators. Both groups require specific encouragement and help as they attempt to display aspects of their classroom practice.

The field-testing of the Resource Pack saw some interesting approaches to implementation at the pre-service stage. In India, for example, our colleagues explored ways of using the opportunities provided by teaching practice. These ways of working were seen as a means of influencing the practice of college tutors as well as the student teachers.

Briefly their model of working was as follows:

1. Outside consultants teach student teachers using sections of the Resource Pack. Initially these sessions are observed by the col-

lege tutors. Later college tutors and outside consultants team-teach during some sessions.

2. Then the outside consultants and college tutors assist student teachers in trying out active learning approaches with classes in local schools.

3. Finally, all are involved in debriefing these practice sessions.

Subsequently, similar activities have been extended to include experienced teachers in the participating schools. In this way, reforms in teacher education and strategies for school improvement are undertaken together in a mutually supportive way, an approach recommended recently by Goodlad (1992).

A number of schools in different parts of the world have been using the Resource Pack as a basis for developing their policies and practices. This is arguably the most powerful implementation strategy. Where all the teachers in a school are engaged in a common exercise of review and development, including built-in arrangements for partnership teaching, there is a real chance of significant developments. In the following account Maggie Balshaw, an educational consultant, describes the use of the Resource Pack as the basis of a school improvement initiative:

A school project

Melbourn School responded to the invitation to take part in the project in March 1992. It is a primary school (Roll: 266 and falling; staffing: 10.5 + Head, 3 non-teaching assistants) in a large sprawling village in the south of England. The oldest part of Melbourn School in use dates from 1850 and the building is fragmented in nature. This physical separation has led to a tradition of limited continuity and little sharing of classroom and curriculum practice in the past.

The headteacher and staff identified the need for a comprehensive reconsideration of the teaching and learning strategies currently in effect was necessary as a response to those children seen as having special educational needs. Indeed the school was viewing the special needs task as a focus for the consideration of the effectiveness of the teaching of *all* children.

In agreeing to work with the school on this initiative I negotiated a contract that attempted to clarify our expectations. This contract stated that the *school* would:

- prioritize in the school's development plan the improvement of classroom practice as a means of improving the quality of education for all pupils;

- allocate the equivalentof three days of staff development (school-based) over the initial year of the project, 1992–93;

- release fifty per cent of the teaching staff from their timetable to engage in paired teaching for a minimum of six sessions during the year (i.e. working together in each others' classrooms in order to implement new approaches);

- nominate three school representatives (two of whom are heads of departments) to attend staff development workshops using the UNESCO Pack and act as co-ordinators of the work in school;

- engage in a process of evaluation of both the processes involved and outcomes achieved.

In return I, as the external consultant, agreed to provide the equivalent of seven days training and support to the school co-ordinators; visit the school on a regular basis; assist the school with planning, implementation and evaluation activities; and provide material support in the form of the UNESCO Pack and videos, along with guidance in their use.

The role of the school co-ordinators has been central to the development of the work. As the head of department (junior), the head of department (infant) and co-ordinator for special needs, they occupy strategically significant roles in the structure of the school.

Their response to the task has been positive, thoughtful and constructive. This response began to take shape during the first three days of workshop activities held during June and July 1992. Initially their task was to identify clearly what role they should play within the project development. They decided that they would be known as the 'Initial Learners', as this seemed an apt description of their perceived task.

The Resource Pack was used during this time to consider the stated needs of the school and match the available and appropriate staff development activities to these needs. The first element of this was to hold a whole school staff meeting at the end of the summer term to inform everyone of progress and planning to date.

The strategic plan had two main elements. The first of these was the process through which everybody in the school was to be drawn into the learning activities that were to take place. The second element was the action plan for carrying out the agreed programme of staff development.

The following strategies were planned:

Whole staff formally:

- occasional staff meetings
- staff development days (October 1992 – using the following pack materials: Unit 1.5 Children's learning and Unit 3.6 Co-operative learning)

Initial learners:

- acting as initiators, resources evaluators and co-ordinators.

Partnerships:

- Three pairs of people, each including an initial learner, involved in classroom partnership (using pack materials: Unit 3.2 Making learning meaningful and Unit 3.7 Structuring group activities
- Six (three pairs) sharing experiences of classroom partnerships.

Departments:

- Infant department: using Module 3
- Junior department: using Unit 3.1 Assessing and recording progress.

Individuals:

- Choosing resources to develop practice in individual classrooms (e.g. Unit 3.7 Structuring group activities).

The most crucial element of this learning process was seen as that of the classroom partnerships. Early indications of the outcomes of this work are extremely positive, even at the joint observation stage and before the planned programme was carried out. The process of getting together and identifying the focus of the planned development in both partnerships and departmental work has had positive outcomes. It must be remembered that there was little experience of classroom sharing and joint planning for this type of activity in the school, so this starting point is very significant.

The first staff development day in October 1992 was a positive and rewarding experience for all the participants. Its aims and framework were planned by the initial learners and everyone was drawn into an interactive programme. The work that preparation for this necessitated should not be underestimated and involved some staff coming under pressure to be ready.

The different individuals, pairs and groups all took responsibility in some way for presenting and leading a section of the programme. A great deal of creativity and, crucially, commitment to these activities was evident. This was because the topics related optimally to classroom experiences chosen by the participants. As such it was an enlightening experience for the school as a whole. Attending the day were non-teaching classroom assistants and a nursery nurse, and they took a full and equal part in the programme.

Evaluation of the project, both formal and informal, is ongoing. For example, the initial learners and consultant are all keeping learning journals. These are seen as an essential element of assessing self-learning, but also recording the shared learning experiences with colleagues.

Drawing up and reviewing action plans for individuals (to meet stated individual learning needs), for partnership work and also departmental developments, is another essential element of the evaluation process. In addition, review meetings are taking place regularly within the school-based programme and involve the consultant on some occasions.

There is an intention to conduct some form of evaluative interviews with school staff in an attempt to assess personal perceptions of the effects of the developments. These will be informal.

At a management level, it is already evident that the active participation and practical support of the headteacher is an important factor in the success of the project. A written report of his perceptions of the project will also be sought.

A public presentation of the developments constituted as the agenda for another staff development day in April 1993. In the interim period, ways were being sought to display progress at an accessible and possibly visual level, such as a notice board or 'celebration' display. This will involve evidence of the children's participation in the project, their work and their learning journals.

Review and evaluation is ongoing and further work on classroom partnerships, drawing in the six staff who had not had personal experience of these partnerships were planned for the first two terms in 1993. Staff meetings, departmental meetings and another staff development day will focus on the work of the various classroom partnerships.

Maggie Balshaw

Evaluation and feedback

Finally, it is important that the introduction of any new ways of working is carefully monitored. In particular we need to know:

- Are we getting anywhere?
- Could things be improved? If so, how?
- How do the people involved feel?

In this sense, evaluation is not a set of scientific principles and complex procedures but simply an attitude of mind. It is about setting aside time to reflect on what is happening, in order to make changes as necessary. It seems so straightforward when expressed in this common-sense way, but it is often overlooked.

In the following account Anupam Ahuja and N K Jangira describe some of the evaluation strategies they are using in their action research project in India.

Evaluating a National Teacher Education Project

This account relates to the national Project in India involving the use of the UNESCO Resource Pack in twenty-two institutions across the country. As mentioned earlier, participants selected and prepared a plan for action research in their respective workplaces. The format followed title of the project, objectives, context, training modality, selection of material and additional preparation data regarding implementation of the project, impact data on teacher attitude to learning and teaching, pupil attitude and class achievement. Different tools to the used for collecting data were also indicated. The design covered baseline data on outcome variables, the context of training, components of the training design and scheduling and post-training data collection and analysis. A task analysis for conducting the action research projects in respective institutions and time scheduling were also worked out.

The action research followed a pre-test/post-test single group research design. School children and teachers were selected randomly. For reliability of the research the participants were made to understand the need to learn together and seek collaboration, and to describe the methods (step by step) and the context. Caution was to be exercised before making conclusions and data were to be reported with examples. The need to triangulate different type of data from interviews, attitude scales, evaluation of proceedings, photographs, audio and video tapes, was stressed. It was also emphasized that there was a need to keep colleagues informed, design a short-term pilot project, seek collaboration, be open to reactions, be self-critical and to have fun as one works.

In order to evaluate the organization and management of training workshops, participants used a daily evaluation sheet, participant questionnaire, group reports, course leader and participants' learning journals, and observations. Course leaders were also asked to note specific reactions to sessions using methods, such as, 'stance taking', 'rounds', etc.

For evaluating the effectiveness of the workshop, measures were adopted to observe changes in the teaching behaviour of teachers, and in children's feelings about learning and teaching in the classroom. This was done using various evaluation measures as follows:

1. Teachers' Attitude towards Learning/Teaching Inventory
2. Pupils' Participation in Learning/Teaching Inventory
3. Classroom Drawing Situation (teachers and children)
4. Learning Preference Questionnaires.

A 'Teachers Attitude towards Teaching and Learning Scale' (TATs) consisting of fifty statements about teaching and learning in the classroom, to be rated on a four-point scale by the teacher, was used. A 'Pupils Participation of Learning/Teaching Inventory' consisted of thirty statements. Children were required to indicate choices as 'Yes' or 'No'.

All the items in the scales were based on the five approaches recommended in the UNESCO pack, and were to be administered before starting and after the project. Scoring was done area-wise in order to observe change. A scoring key, with detailed instruction for use manually or otherwise, was provided for this purpose.

Parts of the pack material were also adapted to be used as evaluation measures. For example, 'Classroom Drawing Situation' and 'Learning Preference Questionnaire' were developed for use in this way by both teachers and children. The 'Classroom Drawing Situation' for children and teachers helps to observe a change in how they viewed their classrooms. Using 'The Profile of the Classroom Drawing', these changes are identified. Criteria for scoring were developed.

'A Learning Preference Questionnaire' consisting of seven incomplete statements on learning was also used. This helped us to observe changes in learning styles in both teachers and children.

Finally, teachers were asked to observe and note changes in their instructional behaviour, and the attendance, achievement and attention span of children after the project and follow-up exercises.

N.K. Jangira and Anupan Ahuja

Some methods of inquiry that can be used for evaluation purposes are outlined in Chapter 5. In addition it is important to pay attention to matters related to 'trustworthiness'. The key issue here is, 'why should anybody take notice of the findings of evaluation activities?'

A number of trustworthiness measures might be appropriate. These include:

1. Provide a detailed account of the inquiry methods used, showing the care that has been taken to get authentic information.
2. Provide a detailed account of the contexts in which information has been collected in order that the audience has a clear sense of what these are like.
3. Take care in reporting information, presenting it in formats that make it easy to scrutinize.
4. Compare information drawn from different sources or using alternative methods. This technique is sometimes called 'triangulation'.
5. Check the information by asking those who gave it to you to check its authenticity.
6. Be self-critical. In other words, keep checking your own interpretations, looking for alternative explanations.

Of course, the central purpose of evaluation activities is to provide feedback to those involved in order that improvements can be made. Consequently it is vital to establish effective procedures for communicating the information that has been gathered.

SOME FINAL REFLECTIONS

At the outset of the UNESCO project that forms the basis of the ideas presented in the book, a number of specialists in special education suggested that the idea of one Resource Pack that could be used in many countries was impossible. Their judgements were that contextual and cultural factors would make the content of such a pack unusable in many countries. In some senses, of course, these colleagues are correct. If we were to develop a pack requiring the acceptance of specific content it would likely only be relevant in a limited range of contexts. This is why our approach has been to emphasize process rather than content. The content offered in the Resource Pack is used to stimulate the creation of responses rather than to encourage the adoption of ready-made prescriptions.

This is arguably the most significant outcome of the research associated with the project. What we have learned is that improvements are most likely to occur when groups of people collaborate together to explore their experiences and understandings. This so often seems to inspire creativity and innovation.

To those readers wishing to develop innovatory projects in education, therefore, the important message is that people matter most. Your best strategy is to create networks of colleagues who are then encouraged to collaborate in making the innovation succeed. They may draw on ideas and even materials from elsewhere, but the basis of improvement is their own combined efforts. In my view this message applies with respect to national, district or college and school-based initiatives.

As far as the 'Special Needs in the Classroom' initiative is concerned, we will continue to build upon this simple idea as we expand the work of the project in further communities. We will do this in the belief that this work has the potential to reform teacher education and, in so doing, improve schooling for all. In this respect we believe that special needs are special in that they provide insights into possibilities for improvement that might otherwise pass unnoticed.

References

Adams, F. (ed) (1986) *Special Education*. Harlow: Councils and Education Press.

Ainscow, M. (1990) Special needs in the classroom: The development of a teacher education resource pack. *International Journal of Special Education 5(1)*, 13–20.

Ainscow, M. (ed) (1991) *Effective Schools for All*. London: Fulton; Baltimore: Paul H Brookes.

Ainscow, M. (1993) Teacher education as a strategy for developing inclusive schools. In R. Slee (ed) *Is There a Desk with My Name on It? The Politics of Integration*. London: Palmer.

Ainscow, M. and Hart, S. (1992) Moving practice forward. *Support for Learning 7(3)*, 115–20.

Ainscow, M. and Muncey, J. (1989) *Meeting Individual Needs in the Primary School*. London: Fulton.

Ainscow, M. and Tweddle, D.A. (1979) *Preventing Classroom Failure*. London: Fulton.

Ainscow, M. and Tweddle, D.A. (1988) *Encouraging Classroom Success*. London: Fulton.

Ballard, K.D. (1990) Special education in New Zealand: Disability, politics and empowerment. *International Journal of Disability, Development and Education 37(2)*, 109–24.

Bassey, M. (1990) Crocodiles eat children. *CARN Bulletin No.4.*

Cambridge Institute of Education. University of Cambridge Institute of Education

Bowman, I. (1986) Teacher training and the integration of handicapped pupils: Some findings from a fourteen nation UNESCO study. *European Journal of Special Needs Education 1*, 29–38.

Carrier, J.G. (1983) Masking the social in educational knowledge: The case of learning disability theory. *American Journal of Sociology 88*, 948–74.

Clark, D.L., Lotto, L.S. and Astuto, T.A. (1984) Effective schools and school improvement: A comparative analysis of two lines of inquiry. *Educational Administration Quartlery, 20(3)*, 41–68.

Crawford, N.B. (1990) Integration in Hong Kong: rhetoric to reality in the field of mental handicap. *European Journal of Special Needs Education 5(3)*, 199–209.

Dyson, A. (1990) Special educational needs and the concept of change. *Oxford Review of Education 16(1)*, 55–66.

Edmonds, R. (1982) Programs of school improvement: An overview. *Educational Leadership 40(3)*, 4–11.

Eisner, E.W. (1990) The meaning of alternative paradigms for practice. In E.G. Guba (ed) *The Paradigm Dialog*. London: Sage.

Fulcher, G. (1989) *Disabling Policies? A Comparative Approach to Education Policy and Disability*. London: Falmer

Fullan, M. (1982) *The Meaning of Educational Change*. New York: Teachers College Press.

Fullan, M. (1990) Staff development, innovation and institutional development. In B. Joyce, (ed) *Changing School Culture Through Staff Development*. Alexander, VA: Association for Supervision and Curriculum Development Yearbook.

Fullan, M.G. (1991) *The New Meaning of Educational Change*. London: Cassell.

Gitlin, A.D. (1987) Common school structures and teacher behaviour. In J. Smyth (ed) *Educating Teachers: Changing the Nature of Pedagogical Knowledge*. London: Falmer.

Goodlad, J.I. (1992) Why we need a complete redesign of teacher education. *Educational Leadership 49(3)*, 4–6.

Goodman, N. (1978) *Ways of World Making*. Indianapolis: Hackett.

Gortazar, A. (1991) Special education in Spain. *European Journal of Special Needs Education 6(1)*, 56–70.

Handy, C. and Aitkin, R. (1986) *Understanding Schools as Organisations*. London: Penguin.

Harre, R. (1981) The positivist-empiricist approach and its alternative. In P. Reason and J. Rowan (eds) *Human Inquiry*. Chichester: Wiley.

Hegarty, S. (1990) *The Education of Children and Young People With Disabilities: Principles and Practice*. Paris: UNESCO.

Heron, R. (1981) Philosophical basis for a new paradigm. In P. Reason and J. Rowan (eds) *Human Inquiry*. Chichester: Wiley.

Heshusius, L. (1989) The Newtonian mechanistic paradigm, special education, and contours of alternatives: An overview. *Journal of Learning Disabilities, 22(7)*, 403–21.

House, E., Lapan, S. and Mathison, S. (1989) Teacher inference. Cambridge. *Journal of Education 19(1)*, 53–8.

Iano, R.P. (1986) The study and development of teaching: With implications for the advancement of special education. *Remedial and Special Education 7(5)*, 50–61.

Jangira, N.K. and Ahuja, A. (1992) *Effective Teacher Training: Cooperative Learning Based Approach*. New Delhi: National Publishing House.

Johnson, D.W. and Johnson, R.T. (1989) *Leading the Cooperative School*. Edina: Interaction Book Co.

Joyce, B., Murphy, C., Showers, B. and Murphy, J. (1991) School renewal as cultural change. In M. Ainscow (ed) *Effective Schools for All*. London: Fulton.

Joyce, B. and Showers, B. (1988) *Student Achievement Through Staff Development*. London: Longman.

Lincoln, Y.S. and Guba, E.G. (1985) *Naturalistic Inquiry*. Beverley Hills: Sage.

Lipsky, D.K. and Gartner, A. (1989) *Beyond Separate Education: Quality Education for All*. Baltimore: Paul H Brookes.

Little, J.W. (1982) Norms of collegiality and experimentation: Workplace conditions of school success. *American Educational Research Journal, 19*, 325–40.

Miles, M. (1989) The role of special education in information based rehabilitation. *International Journal of Special Education, 4(2)*, 111–18.

Miles, M.B. and Huberman, A.M. (1984) *Qualitative Data Analysis*. Beverley Hills: Sage.

Mintzberg, H. (1979) *The Structuring of Organisations*. Englewood Cliffs: Prentice-Hall.

Olson, J. (1989) The persistence of technical rationality. In G. Milburn, I.F. Goodson and R.J. Clark *Reinterpreting Curriculum Research*. London: Falmer.

Pijl, S.J. and Meijer, C.J.W. (1991) Does integration count for much? An analysis of the practices of integration in eight countries. *European Journal of Special Needs Education, 6(2),* 100–11.

Porter, A.C. and Brophy, J.E. (1988) Synthesis of research on good teaching: Insights from the work of the Institute of Research on Teaching. *Educational Leadership, 48(8),* 74–85.

Reason, P. (ed) (1988) *Human Inquiry in Action.* Beverley Hills: Sage.

Rosenholtz, S. (1989) *Teachers' Workplace: The Social Organisation of Schools.* New York: Longman.

Ross, D.H. (1988) *Educating Handicapped Young People in Eastern and Southern Africa.* Paris: UNESCO.

Rutter, M. *et al.* (1979) *Fifteen Thousand Hours.* London: Open Books.

Schon, D.A. (1983) *The Reflective Practitioner.* New York: Basic Books.

Schon, D.A. (1987) *Educating the Reflective Practitioner.* San Francisco: Jossey-Bass.

Skrtic, T.M. (1988) The organisational context of special education. In E.L. Meyer and T.M. Skrtic (eds) *Exceptional Children and Youth: An Introduction.* Denver: Love.

Skrtic, T.M. (1991a) *Behind Special Education: A Critical Analysis of Professional Culture and School Organisation.* Denver: Love.

Skrtic, T.M. (1991b) Students with special educational needs: Artifacts of the traditional curriculum. In M. Ainscow (ed) *Effective Schools for All.* London: Fulton.

Slee, R. (1991) Learning initiatives to include all students in regular schools. In M. Ainscow (ed) *Effective Schools for All.* London: Fulton.

Stainback, W. and Stainback, S. (1984) A rationale for the merger of special and regular education. *Exceptional Children, 51,* 102–11.

Stoll, L. (1991) School effectiveness in action: Supporting growth in schools and classrooms. In M. Ainscow (ed) *Effective Schools for All.* London: Fulton; Baltimore: Paul H. Brookes

Thousand, J.S. and Villa, R.A. (1991) Accommodating for greater student variance. In M. Ainscow (ed) *Effective Schools for All.* London: Fulton.

Tomlinson, S. (1982) *A Sociology of Special Education.* London: Routledge.

UNESCO (1988a) *UNESCO Consultation on Special Education: Final Report*. Paris: UNESCO.

UNESCO (1988b) *Review of the Present Situation in Special Education*. Paris: UNESCO.

Wang, M.C, Reynolds, M.C. and Walberg, H.J. (1986) Rethinking special education. *Educational Leadership, 44,* 26–31.

Wang, M.C. (1991) Adaptive instruction: An alternative approach to providing for student diversity. In M. Ainscow (ed) *Effective Schools for All*. London: Fulton.

Weick, K.E. (1976) Educational organisations as loosely coupled systems. *Administrative Science Quarterly, 21,* 1–19.

Weick, K.E. (1985) Sources of order in under-organised systems: Themes in recent organisational theory. In YS. Lincoln (ed) *Organisational Theory and Inquiry*. Beverley Hills: Sage.

Werner, D. (1987) *Disabled Village Children*. Palo Alto: The Hesperian Foundation.

West, M. and Ainscow, M. (1991) *Managing School Development: A Practical Guide*. London: Fulton.

Will, M.C. (1986) Educating children with learning problems. *Exceptional Children, 52(5),* 411–16.

Yanok, J. (1986) Free appropriate public education for handicapped children: Congressional intent and judicial interpretation. *Remedial and Special Education 7(2),* 49–53.

Achevé d'imprimer sur rotative
par l'Imprimerie Darantiere à Dijon-Quetigny
en avril 2004

Dépôt légal : avril 2004
N° d'impression : 24-0424

Imprimé en France